ADHD
explained

ADHD

Your Toolkit to
Understanding and Thriving

explained

Dr Edward M. Hallowell

CONTENTS

This book could change your life   6

- -

Chapter 1
What is ADHD?   18

Chapter 2
Who has ADHD?   40

Chapter 3
The apple tree of ADHD   52

Chapter 4
A basic plan to live your best life   66

Chapter 5
Time   80

Chapter 6
Money   92

Chapter 7
Doom and gloom   106

Chapter 8
Addiction   122

Chapter 9
Connection and
relationships   142

Chapter 10
Creativity   162

Chapter 11
Careers   176

Chapter 12
Health and wellbeing   184

Chapter 13
Medication   204

~~~~~~~~~~~~~~~~~~~~~~~~~~~~~~~~~~

A final word   214
Resources   215
Index   218
Acknowledgements   223
About the author   224

THIS BOOK COULD CHANGE YOUR LIFE

"I was standing in a bookshop one day, waiting for a friend," Bruce wrote to me, "pulling books off shelves, killing time. For some reason, I pulled your book off the shelf. When I started to read it, the proverbial lightning bolt hit me. I realized that I was reading about myself. Somehow you knew me without ever having met me. It was a revelation, the kind you read about but can't imagine happening to you, only it happened to me that day. I saw myself, my true self, which I'd kept hidden from almost everybody, in your book.

When you described ADHD, which I'd never heard of until then, you described me to a T. It was crazy, all the details you knew about me. You described the ways I was different, but you described them in a way I could actually feel proud of. Just giving me that was huge. The more I read, the more I saw myself. Even though I'd never heard of you or your book, I felt like we'd known each other forever. Somehow, you knew me."

I wonder if I might know you, dear reader, too. If I do, if you see yourself in the descriptions I offer of ADHD (attention deficit hyperactivity disorder), then you are one lucky person. Everything could be about to change.

Undiagnosed ADHD

About 80 per cent of adults who have ADHD don't know they have it. Living your life without knowing that you have ADHD is a bit like being short-sighted without knowing there is a condition called short-sightedness. Once you learn there's a name for why you can't see clearly, you can visit an optician, take an eye test, and get a pair of glasses, and those glasses will change your life in ways you couldn't have imagined because you hadn't known what was wrong or what was possible.

The same is true when it comes to knowing that you have ADHD.

Undiagnosed, ADHD can hold a person back in life. Receiving a diagnosis can change everything.

Keep in mind

Telling someone with ADHD they need to try harder is like telling someone who's short-sighted to squint harder.

Struggling to succeed

Let me tell you about Maria. She is a really good example of how diagnosis and treatment for ADHD can transform your life.

Maria came to see me because she had taken the New York bar exam six times, and she had failed it six times. "I'm smart. I know I'm smart. But I just can't pass this damn exam," she told me. "I had to study three times harder than the other students and I couldn't figure out why, because in class it was obvious I was just as smart as they were, probably smarter."

As she told me her story, it was like she was a poster child for adult ADHD. In the past, when she'd gone for help, she'd been diagnosed with depression and prescribed an antidepressant. She had been depressed for sure, but only because she was so frustrated at not achieving her goals. The drug would not address her underlying problem, which was ADHD.

As I explained this, Maria alternated between crying and getting angry. "Why didn't those doctors see this?" she asked.

"Don't blame them," I said. "Rare is the doctor who knows about adult ADHD, especially in women. But now that we know what's really going on, we can get to work taking care of it."

With the help of stimulant medication and the accommodation of extra time, Maria passed the bar exam with flying colours on her next try.

Fact vs fiction

Fiction:

If you have ADHD, that means you'll never amount to much in life.

Fact:

Almost all of the adults who come to see me underachieved or struggled at school. Many dropped out of school or college. However, they didn't give up. Most started using their natural entrepreneurial talents right away. Aviation pioneers Richard Branson and David Neeleman, innovator and entertainer will.i.am, and model and entrepreneur Paris Hilton are just a few examples of people with ADHD who have achieved great things.

The stakes are high

Not knowing you have ADHD can lead to dire consequences in adulthood, including early death. Russell Barkley, one of the leading researchers in the field, has run the numbers and shown that undiagnosed ADHD knocks off, on average, 13 years from a person's life because of all the bad things that happen to people who have untreated ADHD. The list of adverse consequences includes:

~ high rates of unemployment

~ financial difficulties, which lead to high stress

~ high rates of addictions of all kinds

~ failed relationships, which lead to social isolation, itself a high risk factor for early death

~ depression, which leads to a much higher rate of suicide attempts and completed suicides

~ car accidents

~ injuries of all kinds

~ acute anxiety

~ a spuriously negative view of oneself

~ poor self-care, including putting off follow-up appointments with doctors and dentists

~ underachievement and chronic frustration, which lead to a consolidated sense of loss, the suspicion that you've missed the boat in life, and feeling like a loser

And that's just a partial list!

That list of bad outcomes, some of which are interlinked and fuel one another, may bring a tear to your eye if you have ADHD, or if someone you love has it, but take heart, none of those bad outcomes need happen.

Undiagnosed ADHD knocks off, on average, 13 years from a person's life

Unwrapping the gift of ADHD

We've known about ADHD for several decades but most people, even members of the medical profession, still don't really understand what ADHD is. In fact, many people still believe the caricature of the condition – hyperactive little boys – and have no idea how much more there is to it than that.

Unfortunately, one thing that's slowing the understanding and general acceptance of ADHD is the stigma that hangs over the entire field of mental health. No one wants to think they have a mental illness, and ADHD is unfortunately classified as a form of mental disorder. This medical classification, which I'll discuss in more detail in the first chapter (What is ADHD?, see pages 18–39), ignores all the special talents and strengths that accompany ADHD.

Most people only know about the problems associated with ADHD and don't appreciate that it is a gift waiting to be unwrapped. They aren't aware that many talents and strengths are embedded in this condition, such as originality, curiosity, creativity, vision, imagination, persistence, uncanny intuition, and entrepreneurial drive, to name but a few. You'll learn more about all the positive attributes of ADHD, along with their negative counterparts, in Chapter 3: The Apple Tree of ADHD (see pages 52–65).

I want to share this good news about ADHD with you, the reader. I want everyone to know the upsides of ADHD. Only when this is common knowledge will it be possible to help the millions who still have not found their way out of the maze of undiagnosed and untreated ADHD.

Seeing the beauty in ADHD

Not only is ADHD a gift waiting to be unwrapped, I also like to think of it as a violin waiting to be played. Like the violin, ADHD is a difficult instrument to control but if you practise, practise, practise the skills I am going to teach you in this book, I guarantee you will make progress. Pretty soon you'll be making sweet music in your life, and then you'll be hooked because making progress is habit-forming.

Once you feel the satisfaction of your success, you'll want to keep it for the rest of your life.

It is my life's work to tell as many people as possible the truth about ADHD. I want everyone to know how to get the help they need to turn it into an instrument of beauty – that violin. And if they don't have ADHD, I want them to wish that they did.

How to use this book

I've done my best to make this book ADHD-friendly. You may think that having ADHD and reading a book don't easily mix but this book is different. It's got illustrations, bullet points, and lots of little boxes containing pearls of wisdom about ADHD that I've learned over the past 40 years. You have my word, I will do my very best not to bore you, and, to go one better, I will very likely help you.

This book is intended to guide you through the Land of ADHD, step by step, chapter by chapter. Here's how it works:

Chapters 1–3: I start by explaining what ADHD is in full, both the positives and negatives.

Chapter 4: I introduce a 10-step plan for how to live your best life with ADHD.

Chapters 5–8: I present solutions to some of the most common obstacles in the Land of ADHD: time, money, doom and gloom, and addiction.

Chapters 9–12: I introduce you to four key things that are fundamental for a long and happy life with ADHD: love and connection, a creative outlet, the right job, and taking care of your health and wellbeing.

Chapter 13: Finally, I shine a light on the most useful tool that everyone fears, namely medication.

A promise

If you conclude that you have ADHD after reading this book, I promise you your life will improve. The only question is by how much.

Almost all the adults I've diagnosed since 1981 came to me because of unexplained underachievement. They may have been doing well, indeed extremely well, but deep down they just knew they could be doing even better, maybe *much* better. They knew that they could realize their dreams – dreams they may have been on the verge of giving up on – *if only...*

They just didn't know how to fill in the blank that came after "if only". They didn't know how to fill in that blank because they'd never heard of ADHD. Or they'd heard of it, they didn't know it applied to them.

With proper intervention, careers can leap forward; relationships on the rocks can find safe waters and revive; inner turmoil can subside and peace of mind can be found. Life can improve in every way imaginable.

This is my promise in a nutshell: the diagnosis and treatment of ADHD can turn a life of frustration and failure into a life of fulfillment and joy.

Does that sound too good to be true? It's not. Even if you don't usually read books, give this short one a shot.

This book could make a big difference in the long story of your life.

Chapter 1

WHAT IS ADHD?

ADHD is a befuddling as well as a misleading term because, for starters, we who have ADHD do not suffer from a deficit of attention but rather an abundance of it. However, while this official term is inaccurate you still need to know it, because that's what's used to make a diagnosis. Described in clinical terms:

~ ADHD is characterized by three symptoms:
  - Inattention or distractibility
  - Impulsivity
  - Hyperactivity

~ It is found equally in males and females; it is diagnosed more often in males and underdiagnosed in females because the girls and women who have ADHD tend to be less disruptive and so more easily overlooked.

~ It is often passed from parent to child.

What's in a name?

People ask me all the time, "What's the difference between ADHD and ADD?" Back in 1981, when I first learned about this condition, it was called attention deficit disorder (ADD). Just a few years later, in 1987, the name was changed to attention deficit hyperactivity disorder (ADHD) and the condition was officially divided into subtypes; you could have ADHD with or without hyperactivity. But this division confused everybody because instead of calling one type ADD and the other type ADHD, it was decided to discard the term ADD altogether. Technically, in diagnostic terms, ADD does not exist. Instead, if you have ADHD without hyperactivity, the diagnosis you're supposed to receive is ADHD, primarily inattentive. And if you have ADHD with hyperactivity, your diagnosis is ADHD, combined type. More than 35 years later, this nomenclature still confuses people.

I think we need a new name for this condition because not only is the term ADHD inaccurate, but it also implies cognitive impairments, as if the condition were similar to dementia or, to the ears of the lay person, as if those with ADHD are just not very bright. Therefore, I'd like to propose a new name that incorporates three of the key elements of the condition (variability, attention, and the search for stimulation) into one term: variable attention stimulation trait (VAST). After all, the condition is indeed vast. The term is accurate – one we could be proud to use – and it doesn't make us feel substandard, as if doors are closed to us – which is absolutely not true.

However, for the purposes of this book, to avoid confusion (and an abundance of acronyms) I'll be sticking with ADHD. **But don't forget, those of us with ADHD have a VAST mind.**

ADHD
inattentive

ADHD
combined

ADHD
hyperactive

A trait, a way of being, not a disorder

At the end of this chapter (see pages 35–37) I will show you a more elaborate definition of ADHD from the *Diagnostic and Statistical Manual of Mental Disorders* (DSM). ADHD is one of those disorders. However, in my opinion, the condition is not a disorder, but a trait, a way of being in the world. Depending on how you manage it, ADHD can be a terrible disorder than ruins your life or a superpower that takes you to the top of whatever field you're in. For most people it's a little bit of both. I want to help you maximize the upside and minimize the downside.

So why wait to share that official, more elaborate definition? Well, because after diagnosing thousands of cases of ADHD in people of all ages since 1981, I know what a huge gap lies between what this condition looks like on the open prairie, in real life, and the description of it in the DSM.

Keep in mind

No brain is the same. No brain is best. Each brain finds its own special way.

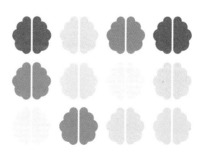

A quick list of ADHD ways of being

Do you think you, or someone close to you, might have ADHD? If you have ADHD, you would likely find that:

~ **Your mind races,** rarely staying in one place.

~ **You can't stand boredom;** the moment you're bored, you're out of there, physically or mentally.

~ **You're original,** marching to the beat of your own drum.

~ **You feel like you are underachieving;** you may be achieving at a very high level, but you know that if you could just find the key you could do much better, and with less effort.

~ **You're impatient,** you *hate* to wait, you just can't stand it when someone takes a long time to get to the point.

~ **You're creative,** coming up with new ideas all the time; the problem is keeping track of them and doing something with them.

~ **You feel a visceral need to achieve things** – to create, to move, to swing into action, to build, to birth something, anything.

~ **You're inordinately stubborn.** (Before you say "no" to this quality, ask someone who knows you well if they think you're stubborn.)

~ **You have a distorted sense of time;** people with ADHD tend to be aware of only two times: NOW and NOT NOW.

~ **You crave high stimulation;** you desire excitement, speed, risk, and instant outcomes. Sometimes people with ADHD fall into the trap of maladaptive ways of getting high stimulation. At the top of the list are all the addictions, to drugs and alcohol; nicotine; gambling; sex; shopping and spending; food and sugar addictions and compulsions; and self-harm.

~ **You hate playing by the rules,** not because you have a problem with authority but because you can see that the most efficient way to get the job done skips over some rules.

~ **You loathe hypocrisy.**

In Chapter 3: The Apple Tree of ADHD I will add more tendencies to this list and you will see how far beyond the DSM it extends. That's because the reality of the condition is vast.

A Ferrari brain with bicycle brakes

I like to compare the ADHD brain to a Ferrari. Like a Ferrari's engine, the ADHD brain packs exceptional power; it goes way faster than the average brain. But there's a problem: this Ferrari brain only has bicycle brakes. A person with ADHD will find it difficult to control the extraordinary power of the brain they were born with.

If you have ADHD, your mind is constantly in motion, revving all the time, wanting to tear away and go as fast as it can. It's mighty tough for any set of brakes to rein in a brain that powerful, which is why many adults with ADHD are so scattered, so all over the place, so here and there and here again, all at once. Power without control creates chaos – powerful, often destructive chaos.

Over the years I've become a pretty good brake specialist. If you have ADHD, my goal is to strengthen your brakes to the point they will slow your brain down when it needs to focus on one detail but allow it to speed up when it wants to go looking for new ideas. The goal is to put you, the driver, in charge of your brain, not have your brain control you.

Much of the treatment of ADHD aims to boost control without reducing creativity or the "special sauce" of charisma and originality that depends upon some degree of spontaneity.

It takes careful calibration to find just the right setting on the inhibitory circuits in the brain to prevent major crash-and-burns, or less severe but also damaging careless mistakes or annoying interruptions.

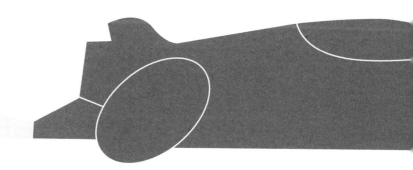

Life before diagnosis

Before you receive a diagnosis, life with ADHD can be one of frustration and underachievement. Ever since childhood you've been lectured that you must try harder, that you're wasting your considerable talent, that you're lazy, and that you'll regret later on that you didn't put in the effort you should have.

Now it's later on. You're starting to lose hope. You know you've been trying hard, but you also know you haven't found the combination to the safe. Success remains locked away and you wonder if you'll ever figure it out.

Let me tell you a true story.

One day when I was just starting to write this book, I ended up stranded at a football stadium carpark, needing a lift. To my surprise, the first car I approached let me in. Sitting in the back seat, I thanked the two young men who'd temporarily rescued me. The driver, Roscoe, asked me about myself. I told him I was a doctor who specialized in ADHD and explained what ADHD was.

After I'd spoken just a couple of sentences, Roscoe said, "That's me! I'm 30 years old and I'm stuck. I'm a really smart guy..." "He's a genius!" his friend interrupted. "...but I'm going nowhere, and I don't even have a plan. I've kinda given up. I don't know what to do, so I guess I'm just waiting for something to drop in my lap."

"Well, here I am!" I said. "Dropped into your lap!" We all laughed, but both guys also took it seriously, as did I. It's why I love my job. I get to deliver good news to people who really need it. I asked Roscoe to read one of my previous books and told him if he saw himself in it, which I was sure he would, then to give me a call. I told him I'd see him for no charge to thank him for helping me.

I hope he gets back to me. But I worry that he won't. You wouldn't believe how many of my sessions with a new patient begin with the patient saying, "I've been meaning to make an appointment to see you for years...".

It's never too late

What I want you to know is it's never, ever too late to be diagnosed with ADHD. I once treated a man who was 76. The treatment helped him to write the book he'd been trying to write his whole life.

The older you get, the more resigned you become, the more you apply words like "failure" or "disappointment" to yourself. But no matter your age, it's never too late. The party called life doesn't end until you're declared dead, and even then, who knows what happens next?

Considering the possibility you might have ADHD and checking out the treatments outlined in this book might turn years of missing the mark and underachieving into victories both in your work and in your personal life.

ADHD and underachievement

The usual tip-off that an adult has ADHD is underachievement. Then you look at the person's history and find out what else is going on. The best test for ADHD is the oldest test in all of medicine: a person's life story.

I have ADHD myself, as well as another widely misunderstood condition called dyslexia. I've had experts in the field tell me that I couldn't have ADHD because I've done too well in life. That's one of the many myths that surround ADHD, that you must be a failure in life in order to warrant this diagnosis.

I'm just one of legions who are living proof of the opposite. I'm a graduate of both Harvard College and Tulane University School of Medicine; I completed my residency at Harvard Medical School; I have a fellowship

in child psychiatry; I've written 21 books that have sold some two million copies; I'm still busy, at age 72, seeing patients every day; and, most important of all, I've been happily married to my wife, Sue, for 34 years, and together we've raised three children, all of whom inherited my ADHD.

But I am small potatoes compared to some of the phenomenally successful people who have these so-called disorders and disabilities. Take a look at the box opposite.

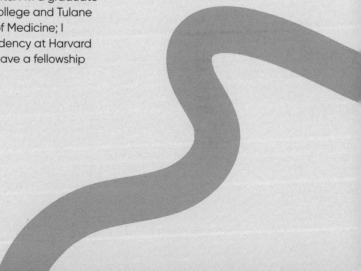

Fact vs fiction

Fiction:

ADHD is just a fancy word for stupid. If you're successful, you can't have ADHD.

Fact:

You name a field, I can name a person at the top of that field who has ADHD. There are Nobel Prize winners in our tent; self-made millionaires and billionaires; successful entrepreneurs of every stripe; world-class chefs, chess masters, concert cellists, comedians, cryptographers, chemists, cardiologists, cartographers, cabbies, and criminalists – and that's just a few of the Cs. We've got every letter of the alphabet represented many times over.

When in doubt, look to the science

Until recently, many people dismissed ADHD as a fad, or an "American invention", as one British psychologist put it to me. He thought it was a made-up excuse for kids who lacked discipline, were lazy, and had parents who wouldn't do what was needed to get their kids to shape up.

Sooner or later, however, science prevails. After all, eventually people accepted that the world is not flat and that the Earth does not sit stationary, like a crowning jewel, at the centre of the solar system.

It hasn't been easy to overcome people's natural bias against ADHD. That's because, on the face of it, ADHD does look a lot like an excuse invented to dodge responsibility.

Let's take a look at a couple of examples:

Teacher

Where's your homework?

Student

I did it, but I left it at home. I have ADHD.

Boss

Why are you late for every meeting?

Employee

I have ADHD so my sense of time is out of sync.

Both those responses are "obviously" poor excuses.

However, just because something *appears* to be bogus does not, in fact, mean it is bogus. After all, what could be more "obvious" than that the world is flat? Or that the Earth is stationary?

ADHD is not an excuse for not taking responsibility. We can't tell the tax collector, "I can't remember to pay taxes because I have ADHD."

We still have to pay our taxes. However, ADHD is a powerful explanation that can help you take responsibility more effectively, such as finding someone to help with your tax returns.

Keep in mind

Living with untreated ADHD is a bit like driving a car with bad windscreen wipers in a heavy rainstorm: you can barely see the road. I like to think that the act of reading this book, which is packed with advice for living your best life with ADHD, is like fitting your car with a powerful set of new windscreen wipers that will help you navigate your future with confidence.

Cultural values have got in the way of understanding ADHD. Western culture, particularly in the UK and USA, puts a high priority on the value of hard work. Our near-reverential belief in the power of hard work all but defines us. The key to success? Work hard. The way out of difficulty? Never give up. In the immortal words of Thomas Edison, genius is 1 per cent inspiration and 99 per cent perspiration.

When ADHD is used to explain away laziness, some people will bristle. To them, this "disorder" is patently fake – an excuse trotted out by people who can't be bothered to be on time, a justification for the laziness of a brilliant student who gets poor grades, or a reason not to fire a supremely talented and imaginative employee who can't be relied upon to deliver on time, blurts out whatever they're thinking, and won't get their act together.

But let's not join the flat-earthers and allow our intuition and common sense to reign unchallenged and supreme, supplanting reason, evidence, and science. Science, after all, is not a system of belief. It is a system of knowledge, of what is *known*. And it is through scientific research that the validity of ADHD was established.

A landmark study in the prestigious *New England Journal of Medicine* in 1990 solidified the position of ADHD on the scientific map by showing a difference in glucose uptake, and hence brain activity, in the brains of adults who had a childhood history of ADHD as compared to adults who had no such history. **The regions of reduced activity in the brain correlated with the symptoms seen in ADHD. So as you can see, science can help us to understand ADHD.**

So what is the official definition of ADHD?

The definition of ADHD in the latest edition of the *Diagnostic and Statistical Manual of Mental Disorders* (DSM) is relied upon by doctors and other clinicians around the world to provide a universally agreed upon definition of the condition. While that definition is limited and reductionist, having such a definition is essential for research, and also to resolve ambiguity as to what ADHD is, and what it is not.

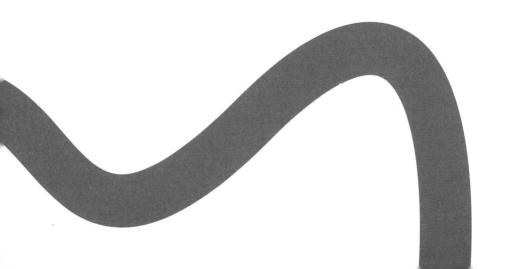

Attention-Deficit/Hyperactivity Disorder (ADHD)
[Definition]

 A persistent pattern of inattention and/or hyperactivity-impulsivity that interferes with functioning or development, as characterized by (1) and/or (2):

1. Inattention: Six (or more) of the following symptoms have persisted for at least 6 months to a degree that is inconsistent with developmental level and that negatively impacts directly on social and academic/occupational activities:

Note: The symptoms are not solely a manifestation of oppositional behaviour, defiance, hostility, or failure to understand tasks or instructions. For older adolescents and adults (age 17 and older), at least five symptoms are required.

a. Often fails to give close attention to details or makes careless mistakes in schoolwork, at work, or during other activities (e.g. overlooks or misses details, work is inaccurate).

b. Often has difficulty sustaining attention in tasks or play activities (e.g. has difficulty remaining focused during lectures, conversations, or lengthy reading).

c. Often does not seem to listen when spoken to directly (e.g. mind seems elsewhere, even in the absence of any obvious distraction).

d. Often does not follow through on instructions and fails to finish schoolwork, chores, or duties in the workplace (e.g. starts tasks but quickly loses focus and is easily sidetracked).

e. Often has difficulty organizing tasks and activities (e.g. difficulty managing sequential tasks; difficulty keeping materials and belongings in order; messy, disorganized work; has poor time management; fails to meet deadlines).

f. Often avoids, dislikes, or is reluctant to engage in tasks that require sustained mental effort (e.g. schoolwork or homework; for older adolescents and adults, preparing reports, completing forms, reviewing lengthy papers).

g. Often loses things necessary for tasks or activities (e.g. school materials, pencils, books, tools, wallets, keys, paperwork, eyeglasses, mobile telephones).

h. Is often easily distracted by extraneous stimuli (for older adolescents and adults, may include unrelated thoughts).

i. Is often forgetful in daily activities (e.g., doing chores, running errands; for older adolescents and adults, returning calls, paying bills, keeping appointments).

2. Hyperactivity and impulsivity: Six (or more) of the following symptoms have persisted for at least 6 months to a degree that is inconsistent with developmental level and that negatively impacts directly on social and academic/occupational activities:

Note: The symptoms are not solely a manifestation of oppositional behaviour, defiance, hostility, or a failure to understand tasks or instructions. For older adolescents and adults (age 17 and older), at least five symptoms are required.

a. Often fidgets with or taps hands or feet or squirms in seat.

b. Often leaves seat in situations when remaining seated is expected (e.g. leaves his or her place in the classroom, in the office or other workplace, or in other situations that require remaining in place.

c. Often runs about or climbs in situations where it is inappropriate. (Note: In adolescents or adults, may be limited to feeling restless.)

d. Often unable to play or engage in leisure activities quietly.

e. Is often "on the go," acting as if "driven by a motor" (e.g. is unable to be or uncomfortable being still for extended time, as in restaurants, meetings; may be experienced by others as being restless or difficult to keep up with).

f. Often talks excessively.

g. Often blurts out an answer before a question has been completed (e.g. completes people's sentences; cannot wait for turn in conversation).

h. Often has difficulty waiting his or her turn (e.g. while waiting in line).

i. Often interrupts or intrudes on others (e.g. butts into conversations, games, or activities; may start using other people's things without asking or receiving permission; for adolescents and adults, may intrude into or take over what others are doing).

B. **Several inattentive or hyperactive-impulsive symptoms were present prior to age 12 years.**

C. Several inattentive or hyperactive-impulsive symptoms are present in two or more settings (e.g. at home, school, or work; with friends or relatives; in other activities).

D. There is clear evidence that the symptoms interfere with, or reduce the quality of, social, academic, or occupational functioning.

E. The symptoms do not occur exclusively during the course of schizophrenia or another psychotic disorder and are not better explained by another mental disorder (e.g. mood disorder, anxiety disorder, dissociative disorder, personality disorder, substance intoxication or withdrawal).

Specify whether:

~ **Combined presentation:** If both Criterion A1 (inattention) and Criterion A2 (hyperactivity-impulsivity) are met for the past 6 months.

~ **Predominantly inattentive presentation:** If Criterion A1 (inattention) is met but Criterion A2 (hyperactivity-impulsivity) is not met for the past 6 months.

~ **Predominantly hyperactive/impulsive presentation:** If Criterion A2 (hyperactivity-impulsivity) is met but Criterion A1 (inattention) is not met over the past 6 months.

Specify if:

In partial remission: When full criteria were previously met, fewer than the full criteria have been met for the past 6 months, and the symptoms still result in impairment in social, academic, or occupational functioning.

Specify current severity:

~ **Mild:** Few, if any, symptoms in excess of those required to make the diagnosis are present, and symptoms result in only minor functional impairments.

~ **Moderate:** Symptoms or functional impairment between "mild" and "severe" are present.

~ **Severe:** Many symptoms in excess of those required to make the diagnosis, or several symptoms that are particularly severe, are present, or the symptoms result in marked impairment in social or occupational functioning.

The Martian test

This chapter started with a question: What is ADHD? Imagine that a Martian walked up to you right now (I know, it happens every day, doesn't it?) and told you it had heard some human talking about ADHD and wanted to know what it is. How would you reply?

If you can use your own words to explain ADHD, rather than reciting the official definition, then you're on your way to an understanding of ADHD that will bring you closer to the ever-shifting reality of your unique way of being in the world.

Chapter 2

WHO HAS ADHD?

Once you get the gist of what ADHD is, a new world opens up for you. You start seeing ADHD everywhere. Not only in yourself but in many of the people around you. Put simply, a whole lot more people, especially adults, have this condition than know they have it.

Once you "get it", and if you read this book you'll quickly "get it", you'll see lots of talented, interesting people in a whole new light, especially high-octane people, people who are creative but not making full use of their talents, and talented people of all ages who are somehow "stuck".

You will likely see it in greater numbers than the epidemiological studies support.

How common is ADHD worldwide?

Since ADHD is one of the most studied conditions in all of medicine, there are dozens of studies on the prevalence of ADHD worldwide. Most of the studies converge on a 5.29 per cent prevalence of ADHD worldwide – let's call it 5 per cent. There are some slight differences between North America compared to Africa and the Middle East, but no significant difference between North America and Europe. What differences there are stem from methodological differences, including variance in diagnostic criteria, the criteria used to assess impairment (a requirement for diagnosis) as well as the sources of the information that was collected.

Five per cent is a significant number for a medical condition. However, as someone who's been learning about and treating ADHD for a long time, I can tell you the prevalence of people who have significant symptoms of the condition, as well as the gifts that so often accompany it, and so would benefit from getting help, is no mere 5 per cent. I'd estimate that it is more like 25 per cent and a recent Mayo Clinic study supports that number.

The prevalence of a version of ADHD that does not meet the DSM diagnostic criteria but is still well worth treating is way higher than the 5 per cent worldwide prevalence of the condition as defined in the DSM.

Put differently, clinically significant ADHD is more widespread worldwide – 25 per cent at least – than the ADHD that meets the DSM criteria.

Studies agree there is a 5% prevalence of ADHD worldwide

However, it's likely that at least 25% of people have significant symptoms

A brief history of ADHD

Most people think of ADHD as a modern discovery, if not an invention. Not so. While the name is relatively new – the term ADHD became the official name in 1987 – the symptoms are as old as humanity.

400 BCE

Descriptions of what we might now call ADHD can be found in the writings of the father of medicine, the Greek physician Hippocrates. He thought the condition was due to an imbalance of fire over water, and for treatment he recommended drinking a lot of water.

1600s

The philosopher John Locke, who also happened to be a physician, wrote in one of his essays on education about some children who could not "keep their mind from straying".

1798

In 1798, another physician, Alexander Crichton, described what he called a "disease of attention", which matched the condition we see today.

1800s

Throughout the nineteenth century, medical textbooks picked up on this theme and gave various colourful names to the condition, including "hypermetamorphosis", "simple hyperexcitability", or "nervous child".

1937

A big turning point came in 1937, when physician Charles Bradley gave the boys on his ward amphetamine. In minutes the children had settled down and started to learn the arithmetic that they'd simply been unable – not unwilling – to learn before. At that time, the diagnostic term commonly used was "hyperkinetic reaction of childhood".

1902

In 1902, paediatrician George Still gave a series of lectures describing what he called an "abnormal defect of moral control". It was ADHD. Sadly, Still's use of the word "moral" reinforced the mistaken belief that ADHD is a moral defect, a product of weak character, that can be fixed by trying harder or through punishment.

1981

By the time I learned about this marvellously interesting condition in 1981, it had been renamed attention deficit disorder (ADD).

1987

Only in 1987 did we start to call the condition ADHD, the name still in use today.

Who is being diagnosed? And who isn't?

The official diagnostic manual, the DSM-3, which was published in 1980 states, regarding what was then called ADD, "the disorder is ten times more common in boys than in girls". However, a 2019 study found the diagnosis of ADHD-based symptoms of inattention was actually more common in girls than in boys, while including symptoms of impulsivity and hyperactivity made it more common in boys than in girls.

Today, the ratio of males diagnosed to females is about 2:1. However, I think that the true ratio is closer to 1:1. That's because females, both girls and adult women, tend not to show the disruptive symptoms of hyperactivity and impulsivity – quite the opposite, in fact – and therefore the diagnosis of ADHD gets missed altogether.

To this day, by far the largest undiagnosed group is adult women. Adult ADHD expert Len Adler estimates that 80 per cent of adults who have the condition don't know it, and so receive no treatment. Far from being overdiagnosed, among adults, especially women, ADHD is vastly

80% of adults who have the condition don't know it

underdiagnosed. If a woman should seek treatment, nine out of ten times she'll be diagnosed with depression or anxiety or both, and put on an antidepressant, which is not what she needs.

According to a 2019 study, diagnosis in adults is catching up with diagnosis in children; four times more adults were diagnosed in the period studied than children. Even so, most adults who have ADHD never get the benefits of diagnosis and treatment.

Keep in mind

It's important not just to get a diagnosis of ADHD, but to get an entire diagnosis. Rarely does ADHD occur by itself. In my own case, I have dyslexia in addition to my ADHD. Anxiety, depression, and behavioural problems are not uncommon, as are addictions and substance use disorders, which I discuss in Chapter 8: Addiction (see pages 122–141).

What if you only have a few symptoms of ADHD?

If you read the DSM-5 definition of ADHD printed at the end of Chapter 1 (see pages 35–37), you'll have learned that to qualify for a diagnosis of ADHD children need six out of nine symptoms listed under the headings inattention or impulsivity and hyperactivity, or both, while adults and adolescents age 17 or over only need five out of nine.

But what if you have fewer symptoms? Strictly speaking, you wouldn't have ADHD. The DSM must set a cutoff number for researchers to do their work, so that one researcher's definition of ADHD matches up with all the others. In research, you must be definite – rigid, if you will – about that. There's no wiggle room or fudge factor. Science requires precision. But we who *treat* ADHD, rather than conduct studies on it, don't need to be so literal, so rigid, so strict.

For example, it can be difficult to decide whether a primary diagnosis is depression, an anxiety disorder, bipolar disorder, or ADHD. The boundaries of those diagnoses often blur together. Sometimes, we end up diagnosing all four. Similarly, it can be difficult to tell post-traumatic stress disorder (PTSD) from ADHD, or primary substance use disorder, or dysthymia (a fancy term for being chronically unhappy). Once again, we may end up diagnosing all four. But maybe the most difficult distinction of all to make – what's called differential diagnosis, weighing the possibilities before deciding on one or more – is telling a severe case of modern life from actual, genetically transmitted ADHD.

So, if you only have five rather than six symptoms, does that mean I wouldn't treat you?

No, not at all. I treat patients, not textbooks. While I wouldn't diagnose you officially with ADHD, and write that diagnosis into your record, I'd work with you to fix whatever is bothering you, leaving the arguments about diagnosis to the academics.

My mission and goal are the same as yours: for you to live the best life you possibly can. So, if you are reading this book and think only a couple of the symptoms apply to you, I think you will still find it useful.

CONFUSED

Blurry boundaries

The boundaries of a diagnosis can blur together, especially when diagnosing the mind. When it comes to human nature, it's impossible to say where the Land of ADHD leaves off and the Land of Anxiety begins. They're not separate countries. They overlap.

Instead of a map with clearly defined boundaries, a better model to describe mental health might be colours. After all, colours can overlap and blend into one another. And what happens when you start mixing colours, or emotions? Sometimes you get great art, other times you get a mess. The point is that a colour model would provide us with a more subtle and individualized way of describing human nature and diagnosing its disorders.

For example, we could say, "Roger suffers from major depression, coloured by frequent episodes of anger,

deepened by his intense fear of death." And then we could add in additional shades for shame, guilt, or alienation. For instance, we could say, "Roger's latest episode of depression was triggered when he entered the hotel room. The unfamiliarity of everything in the room, from the bedclothes to the stark overhead light to the flimsy curtains, filled him with feelings of not fitting in, which instantly drained him of hope and energy."

All of this paints a subtle picture of Roger's state of mind. You can see how readily more colours could be added, say, envy, jealousy, competitive feelings, pity, longing, yearning, and regret. But for our purposes here in describing ADHD, I just want to take you away from the reductionistic world of the DSM and introduce you to the endlessly varied world of actual ADHD.

GRIEVING

LOVING

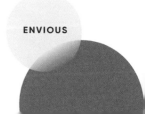

ENVIOUS

SAD

AFRAID

What are the colours of your ADHD?

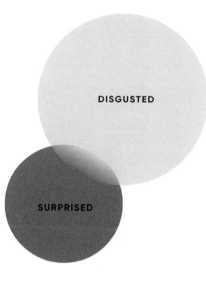

DISGUSTED

SURPRISED

Just as no two people are alike, no two cases of ADHD are the same, though there are commonalities that we share, which come in pairs, one positive and one negative. You will learn more about these paired commonalities in the next chapter.

I encourage you to begin painting your own version of who you are, colouring the various elements or traits that make you who you are in whatever shades and tones fit you.

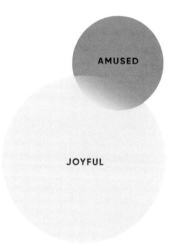

AMUSED

JOYFUL

HAPPY

RELAXED

Chapter 3

THE APPLE TREE OF ADHD

In this chapter, I am going to introduce you to an aspect of ADHD that not a lot of people know about. To get us started, I'd like you to visualize an apple tree. Imagine a tree that's been harvested many times and climbed on by countless children. Picture a well-branched tree, each branch covered with clusters of bright green leaves and juicy red apples that are just begging to be picked. Those apples are going to help me illustrate an important truth about ADHD. It's a fact I learned the old-fashioned way, by listening to people tell me about themselves.

The important truth is this: ADHD is comprised of opposite pairs of attributes. Every positive trait is paired with a negative one. That's why ADHD is neither entirely a blessing nor a curse; it's always a bit of both.

The positive and negative attributes of ADHD

Take another look at that apple tree you visualized. If you look closely, you'll see that each juicy red apple is labelled with a positive attribute that often accompanies ADHD, such as curiosity or creativity. However, if you look closer still, you'll notice that each apple also features a warning that cautions you about a worm that's found its way inside the fruit.

Those worms inside the apples represent the negative attributes that accompany the positive, together making opposing pairs. My job is to show you how to eat each apple without biting into the worm.

Keep in mind

To get what ADHD is all about you need to be aware that every downside has an upside. Every one of our negatives has a corresponding – just as powerful, if not more powerful – positive. For example, the upside of distractibility is curiosity. And what is creativity if not impulsivity gone right?

To get started, let's take a look at each pair of attributes – the apple's blessing and its worm. As you read through this list you will start to form a composite idea of what a person with ADHD looks like. Maybe that person looks like you, or someone you know.

Positive attribute	Negative attribute
Curious	Distractible
Creative	Impulsive
Energetic	Hyperactive
Unconventional	Resists following rules
Persistent	Stubborn
Original	Daft
Great (but selective) memory	Forgets those things that aren't of interest
Loyal	Can be loyal to the wrong person or cause
Full of ideas	Has trouble organizing ideas
Hyperfocused when interested	Mind wanders when not interested
Flourishes in high-stress and high-stimulation environments	Spaces out without high stimulation
Thrives with structure	Resists structure

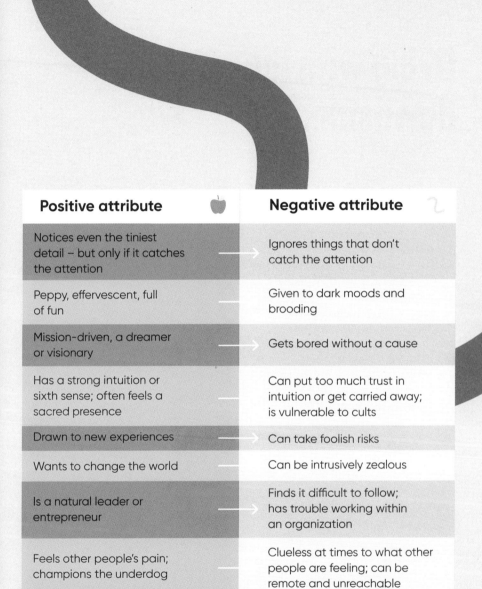

Positive attribute	Negative attribute
Notices even the tiniest detail – but only if it catches the attention	Ignores things that don't catch the attention
Peppy, effervescent, full of fun	Given to dark moods and brooding
Mission-driven, a dreamer or visionary	Gets bored without a cause
Has a strong intuition or sixth sense; often feels a sacred presence	Can put too much trust in intuition or get carried away; is vulnerable to cults
Drawn to new experiences	Can take foolish risks
Wants to change the world	Can be intrusively zealous
Is a natural leader or entrepreneur	Finds it difficult to follow; has trouble working within an organization
Feels other people's pain; champions the underdog	Clueless at times to what other people are feeling; can be remote and unreachable
Fervently desires to be free	Has trouble accepting authority
Needs to build, to create, to grow things	Gets depressed without a creative outlet

Living with the downside

In my experience, women who have ADHD were often quiet at school, dreamers lost in their thoughts; they may have done well by working extra hard at their studies or they may not have done well. In contrast, men who have ADHD most likely struggled in school and felt misunderstood (because they were) and if they continued to university they often dropped out, fed up with the frustrations of education. Of course, some people who have ADHD graduate university and go on to get post-graduate degrees but many more quietly give up on their dreams.

In all genders there's a long-standing pattern of not being understood by parents, teachers, or just about anyone else – even themselves. The frustration and underachievement that people with ADHD experience takes a severe toll on self-esteem, often leading to depression, bouts of anxiety, self-medication with alcohol or other drugs, or compulsive/addictive activities like gambling, sex, or spending. Many, if not most, people with ADHD find ways to compensate for the problems they encounter and manage to get by – often extraordinarily well – but at what price?

Life being what it is, as time goes by the negatives draw more and more attention, time, and money. For those who are married or in relationships, these issues can turn into a daily struggle, each partner wondering where the good times went and what exactly went wrong. Hope wanes.

The same pattern can show up at work. The individual with ADHD is praised for their talent and potential while simultaneously getting closer and closer to losing their job because of underperformance.

Most adults who come to see me have already gone through several jobs, even careers, or have given up and settled into a holding pattern, papering over the cracks and white-knuckling daily life to avoid sinking into the pool of doom and gloom they're living next to.

Without help or the great good luck of finding an extraordinary partner or spouse, the downhill pattern usually continues, the individual keeping it a secret for as long as possible. We folks who have ADHD tend to be very proud. We seem to think it is better to suffer in solitude than show our wounds and get help.

It is puzzling how many people, whether they have ADHD or not, choose to live out their lives in their own private hell rather than let other people in and – through the power of genuine connection – turn that hell into a haven, even a kind of heaven.

The gifts we ignore

Hidden among all those problems, however, are the talents (those positive attributes). They are almost always there, although they may recede as a person gets older. Those of us with ADHD need to identify and mine our talents before they disappear altogether.

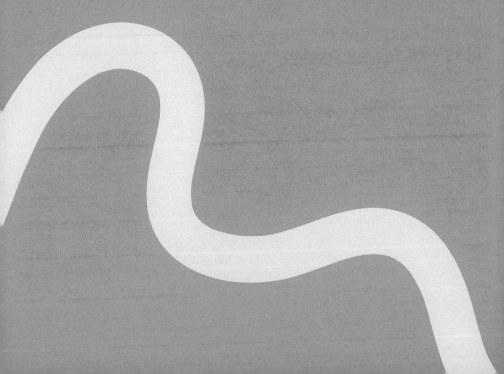

Holding on by our fingernails, we risk losing touch with the talents that could restore us and lead us to a fulfilling and successful life, both in work and in love. Those gifts include a bountiful imagination, bursting with ideas, plans, hopes, and schemes. People with ADHD also tend to be industrious, creative, original, and willing to go out on a limb. We are often strong-willed to the point of being stubborn but at the same time ready to stop and help anyone or to work for a cause until we fall over in fatigue. We are a mission-driven group.

Finding our own mission often marks the turning point when our life starts to take off in a good way.

Our love of high stimulation can serve us well, say in a courtroom or an operating theatre. We love the feeling we get when we can rescue someone in danger or distress. That's the reason why you'll find so many people with ADHD in the healing professions or in high-stimulation lines of work such as being a firefighter. However, our ADHD can also lead us to act blindly or fall in love with the wrong person.

We're drawn to any activity, person, job, career, situation, or means of transportation that combines high stimulation and structure. When I talk about high stimulation I mean danger, excitement, risk, or the chance of a disaster (think extreme sports, fast cars, money speculation, for example) or an instant outcome (like a scratch card, speed dating, or taking a test that gives your score immediately).

High stimulation and structure

What does this combination of high stimulation and structure look like in the real world? Well, imagine racing a bobsleigh, an exhilarating sport that combines speed and skill with the unpredictability of the terrain that lies ahead.

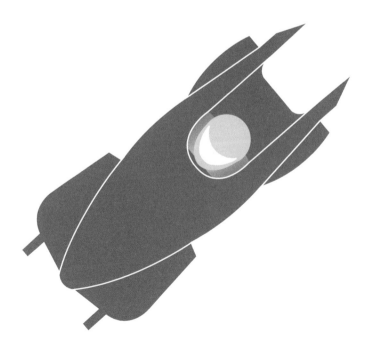

The speed and the danger of bob-sleighing supply high-stimulation aplenty while the walls of the bobsleigh run, as well as the design of the sleigh itself and the rules of the sport, supply the structure.

People with ADHD thrive in situations that combine those two elements but they don't do well when one or both of these elements are missing and can't be added. Put someone with ADHD in the middle of an unexpected crisis – say a house on fire – and they will quickly create the structure they need to evacuate the building and preserve all the belongings that can be saved, while helping the fire brigade do their job as well.

However, put that same person on a beach in the Caribbean and, while everyone else is relaxing and loving it, our poor ADHD fellow will be racked with boredom and feel lost due to a lack of structure. It's only a matter of time before they find their way to a casino where they can find all the structure and stimulation they could ever want.

Keep in mind

Don't fight structure as if it were a controlling boss or a critical parent. Structure shows you a way to get through your day and saves you having to make dozens of trivial decisions, freeing you up to do interesting work.

What does all this mean for me?

What I mean to convey through all these analogies and examples is the amazing blend of positives coupled with negatives that combine in ADHD. Some people paint ADHD as all bad, all pathology, while others overlook all the negatives and focus only on the advantages that come with ADHD.

Both approaches miss the truth: ADHD is an amalgamation of advantages and disadvantages not seen anywhere else in our classifications of human experience, be they called disorders or gifts. ADHD is neither a disorder nor a gift. Rather, it is both.

Whether you end up loving this condition or hating it – and you'll probably feel a little bit of both – what's most important is for you to see how having ADHD plays out in real life.

That's what we are going to do throughout the rest of the book, starting with some practical advice about how to live your best life with ADHD in the next chapter.

Chapter 4

A BASIC PLAN TO LIVE YOUR BEST LIFE

I want everyone to know the secret to living their best life with ADHD. So, what is the magic formula, I hear you ask? Well, here is my 10-step plan:

1. Learn about ADHD
2. Find an ADHD expert
3. Find a coach
4. Create structure
5. Create a lifestyle checklist
6. Find someone to talk to
7. Connect with people
8. Find the right job and the right romantic partner
9. Find a creative outlet
10. Consider a trial of medication

1. Learn about ADHD

Education is absolutely the most important step. Lots of people come to me just wanting to be prescribed medication in the hope that a pill will do all the work. But as the saying goes, "pills don't teach skills". What you need is to learn about ADHD. Knowledge is power, and the power packed into what you learn about ADHD will be the power that opens up a new life for you.

You need to get a feel for what ADHD is like in real life before you drill down into the specific symptoms, traits, and tendencies. I've found that the following metaphors work well when trying to impart the subjective experience of ADHD:

~ Living with untreated ADHD is like driving a high-performance car with bad windscreen wipers in a driving rainstorm.

~ Telling someone with ADHD to try harder is like telling someone who's nearsighted to squint harder.

~ Having ADHD is a bit like trying to break in a bucking bronco. To begin with you may struggle to control it and maybe have some falls. However, over time, you will learn how to take advantage of its strength and power.

Keep in mind

Beware of what you read on Dr Google. There are many self-appointed experts on ADHD, both online and in real life, dishing out wrong information. Most people don't understand ADHD any better than they understand fluid mechanics.

2. Find an ADHD expert

ADHD is a very seductive diagnosis because it resembles so much of modern life. You can see evidence of it in just about everyone. But that doesn't mean everyone has the actual condition. The diagnosis must be made by a qualified professional to avoid diagnosing your entire town.

The best way to determine if a professional is qualified is to ask them how many patients with ADHD they see in an average year. And then you need to break that number down into children and adults.

Of all the medical specialities, child psychiatrists receive the most training in ADHD. Keeping in mind that all child psychiatrists first must qualify as adult psychiatrists, that means the ideal specialist to diagnose ADHD in an individual of any age is a child psychiatrist. However, if you approach a child psychiatrist you should still ask them how many adult patients they treat in an average year because some don't see adults.

Alas, child psychiatrists are as rare as hen's teeth. However, there are many other disciplines that might qualify, depending on the person's experience.

I would recommend that you start with your GP and see who they recommend. Some family doctors have taken an interest in ADHD and become good at taking care of it. Some neurologists have expert knowledge of ADHD, as do some internal medicine doctors. Most psychologists can diagnose and treat ADHD, but most of them can't prescribe medication, although they always have a working relationship with a professional who can.

The point I'm making is that if you do the legwork, you can usually find a suitable practitioner.

3. Find a coach

There is now an entire field devoted to coaching people who have ADHD. An ADHD coach is like an executive assistant. Put differently, an ADHD coach does what your mother used to do when you were a child, minus the nag factor. Your coach acts as your executive function unit – overseeing the complex functions of everyday life – only it's a human outside of your brain doing what your frontal lobes can't quite keep up with.

You can find ADHD coaches easily online. Just be sure to interview them carefully about their experience, especially their experience with someone like you, and also be sure you're a good match in terms of personality, temperament, and style. Ideally, you're going to rely heavily on this person, so you want to be sure from the outset that this is a good match for you.

If you aren't able to hire a professional coach, a friend or family member could do the job just as well, as long as power dynamics don't get in the way. If you choose this option, I suggest using the HOPE method when you meet.

~ The coach begins with **hello (H)**. This is a call to attention.

~ The coach then asks about your **objectives (O)**. What are your three main objectives for today? Just focus on three.

~ Next, the coach asks about your **plans (P)** to achieve those three objectives? Be specific.

~ The coach ends the session with **encouragement (E)**. People with ADHD do much better with a big dose of encouragement.

4. Create structure

Everyone needs structure, or "scaffolding", as some people call it, but people with ADHD are especially in need of it, and they aren't good at creating it for themselves. **To create structure in your own life, you need to build routines, rituals, schedules, deadlines, goals, downtime, work time, and so on.**

Here's an easy way to build some structure into your life, using just a pen and notepad:

~ Start by designating a get-up time and a go-to-bed time. If you stick with it, you will train your brain to get enough sleep. (You'll find advice about improving your sleep in Chapter 12: Health and Wellbeing, page 184–203.)

~ Then list daily, weekly, monthly, yearly, and lifelong priorities. Take your time with this. You don't have to do it all in one sitting.

~ Next, fit each priority or obligation into a daily and weekly schedule, hour by hour.

~ List self-care priorities and schedule them. For example, when and what to eat or when and how long to exercise. As unromantic as this may sound, you might even want to schedule in time to have sex; lots of people with ADHD never do it because they're too busy.

~ Finally, however your plan takes shape, be sure to make time for the things that matters most to you, not just what you must do.

5. Create a lifestyle checklist

You already know the things that should be on a lifestyle checklist: sleep, physical exercise, nutrition, and some form of practice to boost your mental wellbeing, such as meditation or mindfulness. However, you'll need to do more than just "know" the elements of a healthy lifestyle if you want to change your life. The good news is that you will find lots of advice on how to build a healthier lifestyle in Chapter 12: Health and Wellbeing (see pages 184–203).

You may find it easiest to start with just one change you'd like to make. So let me ask you, which element of your current lifestyle would you most like to change? Do you want to lose weight? Exercise more? Get better sleep? Cut back on alcohol or stop midnight snacking? Pick one thing. Just one.

Now, since you are the person most able to make a change in your life, think of a plan that stands a chance of working for you. (A plan you make yourself stands a much better chance of succeeding.)

Set a deadline for your plan. Deadlines work. Trust me. If you don't meet the deadline, extend it. Don't worry or beat yourself up if you miss the deadline you set, and definitely don't give up. Remember, change takes time, and change can hurt, but you will feel *so* much better once you've made that change. Make today the day you transform your life forever.

6. Find someone to talk to

Everyone can benefit from having someone to talk to – someone to listen, empathize, and help you to feel understood. **Feeling understood is a major missing piece in the life of most adults who have ADHD. When you find someone who understands you, it's like finding your way home after a lifetime of feeling lost.**

The person need not be a therapist or a trained professional. In fact, the best people to talk to usually are not. They are friends, relatives, colleagues, even a dog. That's no joke. Dogs are phenomenal therapists.

For example, in my own life, I have a squash game scheduled every other Tuesday with my best friend. We meet at the gym, play squash, and then go to a bar for a few beers. We tell each other everything. Those three hours once a fortnight are invaluable.

See if you can start up that kind of a relationship in your own life.

7. Connect with people

~~~~~~

Connection is the most powerful tool we've got in life to promote pretty much everything that's good, from health, to growth of every kind, to wellbeing, to success, to fulfillment, to joy, to longevity, to happiness, and who knows, maybe to winning the lottery as well. Connected people certainly do seem to be luckier than the disconnected.

Disconnection – feeling misunderstood, overlooked, left out, unable to find a place where you belong – drives most of what's not good in life, from depression, to addictions of all kinds, alienation, anxiety, unemployment, failed relationships, law-breaking, and even suicide.

Connection is the cornerstone of any sound plan on how to live your best life, whether you have ADHD or not, and you'll find a whole chapter about it later in this book (see pages 142–161). Build it into your life. Keep in mind that it is a proven fact that social isolation is as dangerous a risk factor for sickness and early death as cigarette smoking. Plus, connection is one of very few steps you can take to improve your health and wellbeing that's fun, free, and available everywhere.

8. Find the right job and the right romantic partner

If you want to be happy for the rest of your life, commit to the right person and find the right job. Those are your two most important loves. They make all the difference.

The right mate is a person who draws out your best. They are someone who you have fun with and laugh with; whom you respect; who, if you want to have children, you think would make a good partner in parenting; and someone who rubs you the right way, whose jib you like the cut of.

The right job lies at the intersection of three spheres: everything you like to do; everything you're good at doing; and what someone will pay you to do. The more time you can spend there, the happier and more successful you'll be.

You'll find advice about connection and relationships in Chapter 9 (see pages 142–161), and tips on what to look for when choosing a career in Chapter 11 (see pages 176–183).

9. Find a creative outlet

People with ADHD need to create. We need to build, develop, invent, grow, create something – anything – from a business to a boat to a building.

We are born with a unique trait that I call "The Itch". That Itch is in our genes. You'll learn all about the Itch in Chapter 10: Creativity (see pages 162–175), but I mention it here because finding a creative outlet you like and using it regularly is one of the best ways to scratch that Itch.

To find a creative outlet that's going to scratch your Itch, look for something that is both challenging enough that you won't get bored and also exciting enough that you'll want to give it your all. I call this your "right difficult".

More than anything else, our creativity and imagination sets us apart from people without ADHD. But for it to help us the way it can, we need to use it, exercise it, every day.

10. Consider a trial of medication

Medication is the most powerful tool everyone fears. But you do not need to fear it. And it can be a godsend. I am neither in favour of medication for treating ADHD nor opposed to it. What I am is very much in favour of doing whatever will help a person lead the best life possible.

I tell all my patients, let's try anything, as long as it's safe and legal. Used properly, the ADHD medications are both safe and legal, as long as you have a prescription and they're taken under medical supervision.

Stimulant medications, which are the mainstay of the drugs we use for ADHD, will work about 70–80 per cent of the time in a person who has ADHD. The final chapter of this book goes into detail about medication for ADHD (see pages 204–213).

Don't worry, it's all good news.

The thrival instinct

Millions of adults have to manage their ADHD without help. It's a bit like learning how to parachute in mid-air. They're plummeting toward disaster while frantically trying to figure out which cord to pull before they crash. However, I've seen so many people who are plummeting like this "luck out" that I've come to believe there's a special instinct that people with ADHD possess.

You've heard of the survival instinct? Well, people who have ADHD often possess an instinct that goes one better: I call it the "thrival instinct". We don't know how, when, or why it works, nor do we know how to call upon it when we need it, yet, more than any one factor, the thrival instinct is what leads us to achieve at the highest levels.

Once we live to parachute another day, do we spend the rest of our lives in fear of parachutes? No, that's not the ADHD way. Far from running in the opposite direction, we embrace parachutes. Not only do we get back on the proverbial horse that threw us, we show our nemesis who is boss. We proceed to invent a better parachute, one that's foolproof, and sell our idea for a ton of money. And then do we retire and take it easy? No. Instead, we find a way to get into another scrape.

We use our thrival instinct to get out of a problem, and turn that near-disaster into another invention.

Chapter 5

TIME

People who have ADHD don't experience time or feel its passage the way others do. We lack an innate sense of time. We don't know when time is short or when there is time aplenty, unless we're in a high-stress situation that focuses our attention.

This chapter will give you the tools you need to manage time effectively, but first you need to understand how time operates within the ADHD brain.

Do people with ADHD experience time differently?

In short, yes. It may sound implausible but it happens to be true. **For people with ADHD there are only two times: NOW and NOT NOW. That's it.**

Let me give you an example. If you're told that a proposal is due on your manager's desk on Thursday morning and today is Monday your reaction is simply "not now" and the matter disappears from your mind. It reappears only when "not now" becomes almost "now", like late on Wednesday night. Only then and in a panic do you realize the proposal is due the following morning and frantically try to get it done.

Why such tasks come to mind at the last moment is unknown. It's as if people with ADHD have a sort of guardian angel who reminds them about imminent deadlines they've forgotten when there's no time to spare. If you balk at the idea of a guardian angel, you could hypothesize that important deadlines burn themselves into a special circuitry in the brain. Whatever the reason you remember things in the nick of time. When you panic about a remembered deadline your adrenal glands secrete a lot of adrenaline, a hormone that is chemically similar to the medications we use to treat ADHD. **Effectively, without knowing what you're doing or meaning to do it, you're self-medicating with adrenaline.**

Explaining "now" and "not now" to other people

The outside world takes it for granted that everyone has a sense of time. For example, if you agree to meet a person at 7pm they will expect you to arrive at or around 7pm. If you are late regularly, that person may consider your lateness to be a moral failing on your part. Your lateness may count as a strike against you – and in life you only get so many strikes before people stop having confidence in you.

Sadly, most people confuse the world of "now" and "not now" with the world of "don't care" or "can't be bothered" but that's just not true.

If you have ADHD it's important to explain to other people how your brain processes time. I wouldn't recommend telling the types of people who are likely to dismiss it as a weak excuse but do try and explain it to the people you trust and care about.

Keep in mind

It's important to apologize if you are late, but never apologize for having ADHD. Remember, your genius comes from your ability to see what other people can't. The price you pay for that is that you can't always see what other people can. What you can see turns out to be far more valuable than what you can't.

What can you do if you're always late?

This is a tough problem to solve. Almost everyone can learn how to be on time. However, some people will find it extraordinarily difficult. Here's my approach, which is based on my 40+ years of helping people to tackle this problem.

1. Reframe the problem

It's important to stop thinking about timekeeping issues in terms of morality. Punctuality is not a virtue and lateness is not a sin. The solution to chronic lateness does not lie in punishment but in learning how to get around the problems it can create.

2. Enlist help

You'll find it easier to tackle your timekeeping issue if someone else helps you. This is especially true if you've already tried – and failed – to solve the problem on your own. In addition, it's depressing trying to do this alone. When you have help you naturally feel more energized and better able to solve a problem.

3. Take charge of yourself like never before

There's an old saying, "if nothing changes, nothing changes". First, exhaust all the tried-and-tested strategies for poor timekeeping, such as alarm clocks; wristwatch alarms; written reminders; leaving for appointments earlier than you think necessary (I mean WAY earlier, like an hour earlier than you've ever left before); or steering clear of distractions that have made you late in the past, such as stopping to chat, getting coffee, or – the granddaddy of them all – dealing with just one last email. All these strategies fall under the category of "structure". Remember, people with ADHD are especially in need of structure (see page 62).

Be ruthless with yourself, like a drill sergeant. Take no prisoners.

Keep in mind

It's helpful to reflect on the reasons that cause you to be late. For example, one common reason for lateness is the most obvious one: procrastination – you put off what you don't want to do.

4. Consider the reasons behind your lateness

It's possible that hidden reasons may be causing your lateness. For example, being late is one of the most common ways to express anger passive-aggressively. The best way to get at this kind of psychological material is to consult with a skilled therapist. Introspection alone usually won't work because it's all but impossible to do therapy on yourself. If you uncover heretofore covert psychological reasons for your lateness then work with a professional to resolve those issues.

Once you're satisfied that there are no hidden psychological reasons for your problem with punctuality, consider whether you have a different sense of time from most people. If you conclude that you do and you're quite certain it's not a rationalization for not wanting to do something, it's time to figure out what to do about it – the next steps will help you with that.

5. Commit to solving this problem

Building on the strategies in step 3, you need to commit to tackling your lateness as if your life depends on it. You need to get totally psyched to solve this problem because, be honest, one of the main reasons – if not the main reason – for you being late all the time is that whatever you're doing that makes you late is way more interesting than the meeting you're supposed to be on time for.

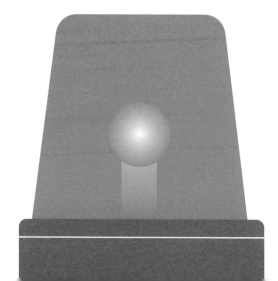

6. Make the solutions stimulating

As I've already mentioned, people who have ADHD are always seeking high stimulation (see page 62). Therefore, I suggest that you tap into that aspect of ADHD and try to come up with some really exciting, novel, maybe even outrageous ways to keep your timekeeping on track. **You need to think of a technique that will grab and hold your attention.**

Below are some admittedly off-the-wall suggestions to inspire you:

~ Buy a siren or very loud alarm and ask someone to set it off 15 minutes before you need to leave to be on time and then again at the exact time you need to leave. (If you choose a siren, you might want to save it for important appointments.)

~ Ask someone (an assistant, a housemate... whoever) to come in and literally carry you out of your office and send you off on your way.

~ Hire a dog walker to include you on their route and pick you up just as if you were one of their pack of dogs.

~ Clear out the 30-minute period before you need to leave to be on time for your appointment and allow yourself to do *nothing* for those 30 minutes. If possible, ask someone to watch over you for those 30 minutes. During that time you must sit in silence, like a child in an old-fashioned detention period. This technique is called aversive conditioning. The idea is that the experience of sitting doing absolutely nothing will be so awful that you will do anything never to have to do it again, though you will have to do it again, *unless* you are on time.

7. Log your appointments

Start keeping a record of both the appointments you're late for and the ones you're on time for. It's been shown many times that keeping a record of your progress at anything improves your performance.

One simple way to boost your chances of remembering appointments is to write them down by hand. Recent neuroscience research has shown that your brain holds more tightly onto what you write by hand than what you type.

8. Get yourself evaluated for ADHD

If you have this much trouble being on time, even knowing that your job hangs in the balance, for example, then there is a very good chance you have the trait so misleadingly called ADHD. If you receive a diagnosis of ADHD, I advise you to talk to your doctor and discuss medication. It can be a game-changer.

However, medication (see pages 204–213) should never be the sole treatment for ADHD. It should always be combined with learning about yourself and your version of ADHD. Don't forget that love and connection, a creative outlet, the right job, and taking care of your physical and mental wellbeing are all fundamental to living your best life with ADHD (see pages 66–79).

Take heart

Take comfort from the fact that people who live in the world of "not now" and "now" usually have an exceptional ability to hyperfocus in the now. In fact, that is one of the reasons why they're so often late. As is the case with every negative tendency in the world of ADHD, there's a positive on its flip side. It's part of what makes this condition so fascinating; it's both a gift and a curse. Our goal is to turn it into as little of a curse as possible and as much of a gift as we can.

Chapter 6

MONEY

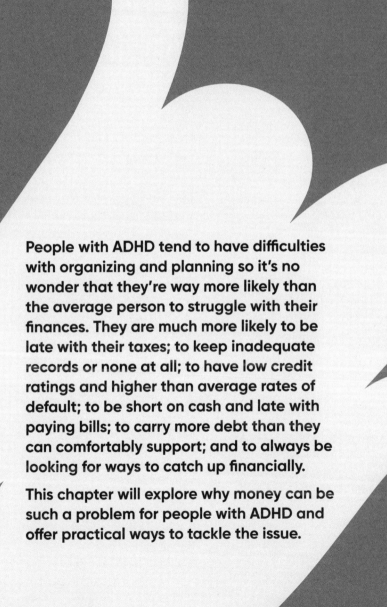

People with ADHD tend to have difficulties with organizing and planning so it's no wonder that they're way more likely than the average person to struggle with their finances. They are much more likely to be late with their taxes; to keep inadequate records or none at all; to have low credit ratings and higher than average rates of default; to be short on cash and late with paying bills; to carry more debt than they can comfortably support; and to always be looking for ways to catch up financially.

This chapter will explore why money can be such a problem for people with ADHD and offer practical ways to tackle the issue.

Why is managing money so difficult for people with ADHD?

People who have ADHD love the excitement of making money (the speculation, the risks, the deals, the wins, and even the losses) but they just can't get into the details – and that's where the problems around their finances arise, almost always.

One of the leading problems in life with ADHD is poor executive functioning (EF). EF refers to the brain's ability to oversee the complex functions of everyday life, much as a chief executive officer oversees the functioning of an organization. We all depend upon our brain's EF to plan, prioritize, organize, gather information and sort it out, weigh probabilities, sweat the details, and keep our lives on track. It's a huge job. At its best, EF comes naturally, instinctively, but almost everyone needs some help to stay on top of things, whether it's a simple list, an online calendar, or a more complex system.

Most people who have ADHD struggle with EF and require help to do what needs to be done in an orderly and timely fashion. (Even that phrase, "an orderly and timely fashion", can trigger a person who has ADHD, bringing back traumatic memories of previous failure and humiliation.)

Managing money well depends upon good EF so it's no surprise that people with ADHD often find money-management to be their Achilles heel. If they're not careful they can end up living a life that takes them from rags to riches and back to rags over and over again. Some people like that kind of life, sort of, but over the long haul it can wear you, and whoever is with you, down, if not out.

Keep in mind

It is not a moral failing if one of your weaker areas is executive functioning and money management.

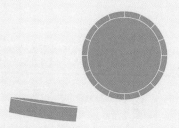

Is there really a link between ADHD and financial troubles?

Let's start by looking at some data. It's frightening – but only if you ignore it. The first systematic study on how adults who have ADHD fare with money was conducted only recently in Sweden. Starting with the mental health data for the entire Swedish population (some 11 million people), the investigators took a random sample of 189,267 people. They then looked at credits and defaults between 2002 and 2015 in that sample, while also identifying people who had and did not have ADHD in the sample. The study confirmed with hard data what might have been predicted.

The people who had ADHD started out at age 18 on a par credit-wise with their peers who did not have ADHD. However, by the onset of middle age the ones with ADHD had fallen into financial trouble: their default rate on loans grew exponentially, their credit ratings declined apace, as did their use of credit in spite of the high demand for it.

Interestingly enough, treatment of their ADHD with stimulant medication had no impact on their problems managing money. This makes sense, actually, because the problems people with ADHD have around money come more from emotions rather than lack of focus. Stimulant medication improves focus but it does not address the emotionally upsetting feelings associated with money.

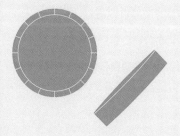

As difficulties with money mounted in the ADHD group, so did depression and even suicide. Stress over money in the group who had ADHD was associated with *four times* the rate of completed suicide compared to the group who suffered financial distress but did not have ADHD.

Put simply, ADHD made everything related to personal finances a lot worse.

And there's more. A recent US study into the long-term financial outcome of children diagnosed with ADHD showed that the lifetime projected earnings of the young adults with ADHD studied was $1.27 million less than the non-ADHD group. Meanwhile, a UK study, which spoke to 506 adults living with ADHD, showed that 65 per cent reported they struggled with financial matters, compared to 37 per cent of those who did not have ADHD. In addition, 76 per cent of the ADHD group reported significant anxiety around money matters compared to 38 per cent in the non-ADHD group, and 31 per cent of the ADHD group reported significant debt compared to 11 per cent of the non-ADHD group.

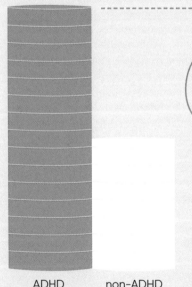

ADHD   non-ADHD

76% of the ADHD group reported significant anxiety around money matters compared to 38% in the non-ADHD group

How do you fix the problem?

If you've read this far you know I'm going to say that the solution starts with education, with learning how you, ADHD, and money interact. After all, knowledge is power. Once you know what's going on you can usually find a way to fix it, or at least improve the situation.

Getting a handle on money, if you have ADHD, is a little like getting a handle on time, which we discussed in the previous chapter (see pages 80–91). When tackling the issue of time and ADHD the most important step is to learn how people with ADHD experience time differently to other people. With money, the most important step is to learn what the topic of money does and doesn't do to your mind and why you have such a difficult time managing it while people who are less smart have no trouble at all.

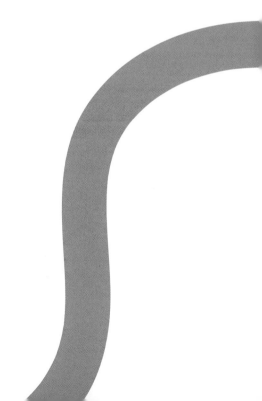

Understanding money and the ADHD mind

Let's start by looking at what money *doesn't* do to us.

Money management doesn't hold the attention of people with ADHD. Money itself certainly holds our attention, in that we all want and need it, but those of us with ADHD would rather watch paint dry than think about the *details* of managing money.

As you know, people with ADHD crave high stimulation. Lack of stimulation (that is, tedium) repels us and that means we find everyday money matters boring, boring, boring. We just can't get into budgeting, saving, managing receipts, tracking credit cards, keeping up with payments, looking for the best deals, and so on. It doesn't matter that these types of tasks are essential, to the point that our lives depend on them, we still ignore, avoid, and deny them because we cannot tolerate the stupor they induce.

Now, let's look at what money *does* do to us.

Money matters make us anxious. Put more accurately, thinking about money matters freaks us out, induces a state of panic, and makes us worry about what the future might hold. And what happens when we get anxious? We avoid dealing with the issue.

So, you see, on the one hand, we are bored by money and tune it out when the topic comes up. On the other hand, we are terrified of the subject, fearing what our ineptitude around money might lead to. If you put these two reactions together you will start to see the problem in a nutshell:

boredom + terror = avoidance and denial

Back to fixing the problem

We can get into big trouble when we use avoidance as a coping style. It's like thinking our dental cavities will go away if we avoid the dentist. I have patients who haven't paid taxes in years, hoping that their tax bills will simply disappear. These are smart people – they *know* the bill won't disappear – but so intense is their fear and anxiety around it that they choose to live in avoidance and denial rather than addressing the problem head-on. It's the same deal with people who avoid the dentist.

Believing you can make a problem disappear by ignoring it and refusing help are dangerous tricks the mind plays on itself.

If the stakes are small, like ignoring the noise coming from a party next door instead of asking your neighbours to quiet down, then it's probably fine, even a good idea, to let the issue go. However, with high-stakes subjects like your health or your financial wellbeing, avoidance can be, as the Swedish study proved, not only the path to worse problems but even to death itself.

Nobody is better at making money than people who have ADHD. We are able to make a lot of money fast, and we can lose it even faster. On the following pages, there is practical advice to help you prevent the losses and other financial problems.

1. Understand the boredom/terror response that induces avoidance

Once you comprehend that your boredom/terror response to money is causing your financial problems it becomes a lot easier to get past avoidance and take action. Just remember, it's your psychology – the working of your mind – that is keeping you from dealing with your money issues, not reality.

Here's the good news: it's possible to redirect your mind and stop it getting in your way.

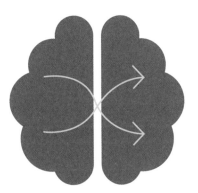

2. Take control of your mind

In order to redirect your mind you need to know the Worry and Anxiety Equation (see below). This equation is of huge practical importance.

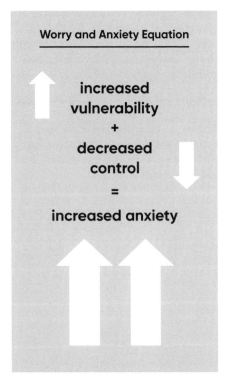

Worry and Anxiety Equation

increased
vulnerability
+
decreased
control
=
increased anxiety

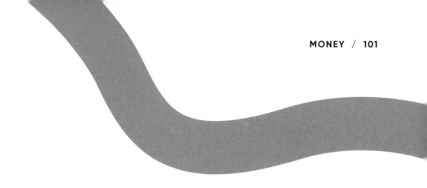

The more that feelings of vulnerability increase and the more that feelings of control decrease, the more that feelings of anxiety rise. I add the words "feelings of" because, believe it or not, the objective, external reality doesn't matter; it's how you feel about that reality that makes all the difference. This is equally true when it comes to money matters, the cold, hard numbers do not matter *nearly* as much as how they make you feel.

Once you understand how your anxiety is causing you to avoid dealing with your financial problems, you need to take action to reduce your anxiety.

Do everything you can to reduce your feelings of vulnerability and increase your feelings of control, reversing the Worry and Anxiety Equation.

Here are some practical suggestions:

~ **Get the facts.** Toxic worry and debilitating anxiety usually derive from wrong information, lack of information, or both.

~ **Get help.** Involve another person in the money-management process, be it a friend, partner, spouse, colleague, bookkeeper, or financial planner. One of my first rules in life is to never worry alone.

~ **Make a plan.** If you have a plan you instantly feel more in control and less vulnerable, even though the external reality hasn't changed. If the plan doesn't work, revise it. Life is all about revising plans.

3. Get help with your EF

Managing money well depends upon good executive functioning (EF) (see page 94). If you struggle with EF, an ADHD coach (see page 70) will be able to teach you these skills. Such coaches are easy to find online.

4. Don't settle for crisis intervention

Your goal ought to be gaining knowledge and the emotional growth that comes with it. Once you find a financial advisor who pulls you back from your money troubles, work with them to develop the knowledge and stability to consider financial matters without immediately needing to change the subject. **Until you gain some degree of confidence around money you'll always be at risk of being taken advantage of financially or not cutting the best deal for yourself.**

5. Don't spend your life trying to become good at managing money

You build the best life for yourself by developing what you're good at, not shoring up your weaknesses. It's up to you to decide what level of financial competence to settle for. Just beware of the very common bad habit that lots of us with ADHD have: a lifelong attempt to get good at what we'll never be good at in a million years.

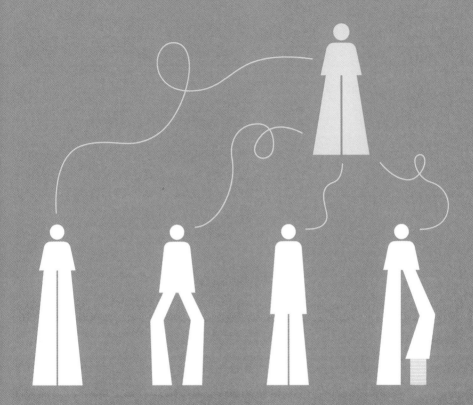

6. Delegate, delegate, delegate

Unless you have a special talent or unusual insight into finances, it's better to delegate your money management to someone you trust – seek help from friends and professionals.

7. Reject shame

Most of the advice you will read about managing your money will encourage you to record all your financial transactions, keep careful records, keep careful tabs on your credit cards, develop a budget and stick to it, and so on. That's all excellent and obvious advice. However, if you are able to do all those things you probably don't have ADHD. The end result of that advice, therefore, is to make you feel even more ashamed and more stupid than you already do because you know you can't do those things.

Stop! Don't let shame take over. Be proud of your talents and your special powers. Don't let the worm eat up the apple!

Take charge

People with ADHD have unusually powerful talents and strengths but they also have weaknesses. Managing money is often one of those weaknesses. So what? As long as you get the kind of help set out in this chapter you'll be fine, indeed better than fine because you will have taken care of one large problem, your avoidance of financial management. Reject shame and charge full speed ahead, powered by your talents and strengths.

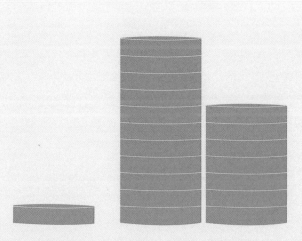

Chapter 7

DOOM AND GLOOM

Of all the problems people experience with ADHD, by far the most painful to endure and the most damaging, ripping self-esteem to shreds each time it hits, is brooding, which I call "Doom and Gloom".

I know this is a tough topic but stay with me, there is light at the end of the tunnel. However, before we get to the things you can do to combat brooding, we need to begin by taking a look at what brooding looks like and why it is a particular problem for people with ADHD.

The toxic effects of negative self-talk

Julian's story

Julian is a journalist. He has been writing newspaper columns for 29 years and still loves his job. Twelve years ago he was diagnosed with ADHD. After getting the diagnosis and starting on medication, every aspect of his life improved, with one exception: his negative inner voice, which would beat him up.

"You suck," it would say, "You're a two-bit columnist writing for a two-bit newspaper. Real columnists write for *The Times* or they write novels. What a joke! What a poor excuse for a writer

you turned out to be. You're just an ageing, over-the-hill hack. You've lost your spark. You're toast, buddy." On and on the voice would go.

These "episodes" – that's what Julian called them – came all too frequently, with no warning or trigger. It was like a form of epilepsy. However, unlike epilepsy, there was no medication to control the episodes. All Julian could do was wait them out, captive in his own mind, listening to that negative inner voice until it petered out, its venom finally spent.

Creativity and mental disorders

What am I supposed to say to patients who torture themselves with negative self-talk? "Well, look on the bright side. I guess beating yourself into a pulp when you're alone is the price you have to pay for being so talented." I'd like to be able to offer them something better than that. And yet, that explanation does appear to be true, even though it's of small comfort to a person in pain.

Most people who have exceptional creative talent, from the arts to business to science, also suffer from one or more of the conditions we diagnose in mental health, including major depression, an array of anxiety disorders, substance use disorders, bipolar disorder, autism spectrum disorder, various character disorders like paranoia, borderline personality, narcissism, and, yes, ADHD.

Why is that the case? Has recent neuroscience advanced our understanding to the point that we have a scientifically valid explanation?

The answer is...(drumroll, please)... yes. Thanks to the work of John Gabrieli, a neuroscientist at the Massachusetts Institute of Technology (MIT), as well as various others, we've learned through functional magnetic resonance imaging (fMRI), a kind of scan that allows us to watch the brain in action in real time, about brain networks and so-called connectomes, groups of neurons that fire together.

The Demon of ADHD

Two connectomes, groups of neurons that fire together, hold the secret to the problem of brooding and those feelings of doom and gloom: the task positive network (TPN) and the default mode network (DMN).

The TPN

is activated when the brain engages in a task that demands conscious attention.

The DMN

is activated whenever the brain is not engaged in a task that demands conscious attention. As its name implies, it's the default state.

I like to call the DMN the "Demon" – not only because when you say the letters D-M-N out loud it sounds a lot like the word "demon" but also because it's the network that sends out all those horrible messages.

Be that as it may, just like everything else in the world of ADHD, there's an upside to that Demon. What upside could there be to a connectome that inflicts the kind of torture – that negative self-talk – we endure, I hear you ask. Well, this connectome is also the seat of the imagination. In fact, the imagination is housed in both the DMN and TPN.

And why is this important? Well, one thing that sets people who have ADHD apart from those who don't is their prodigious imagination. When our imagination operates in the TPN – when it is engaged constructively in a task – it is our greatest ally, our superpower. However, when the task is completed and the TPN shuts down the DMN lights up, and when that happens our imagination becomes our worst enemy as the Demon makes its diabolical rounds. So you see, what we need to do is learn to manage the DMN, not get rid of it.

Finding your flow

Let's drill down a bit further. When you are engaged in performing a task of any kind, from frying an egg to playing the piano to writing a report, your TPN lights up. Your imagination, in the form of the TPN, engages in the task. It becomes *one* with the task. The psychologist Mihaly Csikszentmihalyi named this heightened state of mind "flow".

Flow occurs when your imagination is so totally engaged in what you are doing that you forget everything else. When you are in that state of mind you lose awareness of who you are, where you are, and what time it is. Your imagination, flying on the wings of concentration, transports you to the state where you're at your happiest and where you do your best work. Your entire mind is fired up by your imagination. You're not just following directions, you're innovating, thinking on the spot, changing plans even as you execute them. Your brain is buzzing. It's like a popcorn machine, generating new ideas – pop! pop! pop! all the time. This is how Nobel Prizes get won.

When you are in a state of complete absorption you stop censoring yourself; that is when the impulsivity in ADHD becomes such an asset. Your mind can keep firing up new images, new ideas, new schemes, and new plans with no care as to how ridiculous they might seem to an outsider.

People who have ADHD can access flow more easily than others. They have looser barriers between the TPN and the DMN, which allows them to switch back and forth more easily.

As usual, this is both good and bad. On the good side, we can slip into the TPN faster than others, accessing flow more readily. On the bad side, we can also slip into the DMN faster than others and be taken over by the relentlessly negative messages the DMN pumps out like so much sewage.

Don't feed the Demon

Understanding that you have easier access to the TPN as well as the DMN gives you the precious key to unlock the prison the DMN can put you in.

You don't need to consult with a doctor, or any other professional for that matter. All you need to do is practise one deceptively simple technique: don't feed the Demon.

You feed the Demon by giving it your attention. The moment you deny it your attention – stop "feeding" it – poof!, it shuts down. The Demon can't survive without your attention.

If you want to stop feeding the Demon you need to learn how to redirect your attention. Simple, huh? Instead of looking left, look right. Instead of staring at an accident on the side of the road, drive past it without looking at it. It turns out that's not so easy...

Why is it hard to deny the Demon your attention?

Shouldn't it be really easy to shift your attention away from something that's torturing you? Unfortunately, the reason you keep giving *that* monster your attention is because it is stimulating. One of the first laws of ADHD is that we crave stimulation (see page 62), even painful stimulation and can't endure boredom. Some would say we crave painful stimulation especially. Well, nothing is more painfully stimulating than getting beaten up by the Demon. That's why we keep feeding it our attention.

Why do we choose pain over contentment? Well, the problem with contentment is that it's too bland. That's the trick the Demon plays on us. It takes advantage of our need for stimulation *of any kind* by supplying us with misery, which we strangely can't get enough of.

However, with practice – and it does take practice – you can learn how to redirect your attention or, even better, engage in an activity that's stimulating enough to snatch your attention out of the hands of the Demon.

Learn to look away

To rid yourself of the damage the Demon can do, you need to learn how to redirect your attention away from pain and misery and focus instead on things that are good, kind, generous, loving, beautiful, or sweet.

To help you with this, I want to introduce you to Epictetus, a Greek Stoic philosopher who lived over 2,000 years ago. He was born into slavery and his early life was full of suffering. However, he took what he was given and focused on living the best life he could. What was his secret? He understood that although we can't control the world around us we can control how we respond to it. In other words, the secret to happiness is to control your thoughts, redirecting your attention away from pain and misery and focusing instead on something positive. So you see, my advice has a greater authority behind it than you might have imagined.

In order to control your mind, you're going to need to create some high-stimulation competition for that oh-so-stimulating Demon. You need to choose something that will grab you and draw you in.

Tricks of the trade

Make a list of high-stimulation activities to close down the Demon that suit you. Write it down, keep it on your person, and use it whenever the Demon breaks into your mind.

Here are a few things to consider:

~ **Intense physical exercise** works for most people.

~ **Loud music** – and I mean *really* loud music – competes well with the Demon.

~ **Calling a friend** who you haven't spoken to in a while and getting into the emotions of reconnecting is usually a reliable technique.

~ **Doing a puzzle** also works, though be sure to choose one that is difficult enough to hold your attention but not so difficult that you can't do it.

~ **Screaming** can do the trick too, as long as you're in a place where you can let loose with a real scream.

As I've already said, learning how to redirect your attention takes practice. The Demon is highly skilled at getting you hooked on the pain it inflicts but it is possible to learn how to get rid of it, or at least minimize its impact, once and for all.

Battling the Demon

My story

I have struggled with the Demon ever since I was in high school. For most of my life I have been at the mercy of random, unpredictable dips into bleak despair for which I had no means of repair other than waiting them out. I've suffered from brief but chilling dips into darkness. Those dips have made for some of the loneliest, emptiest moments in my life. In those moments of hopelessness and isolation I felt no motivation to live, or to die for that matter. I felt no desire at all. I knew I'd never take my own life. However, during those moments I wouldn't have minded if my life had been taken from me.

I always ascribed these "episodes" to my erratic and topsy-turvy childhood but I might as well have ascribed it to the star sign I was born under or the phases of the moon. Before my training in psychiatry I had no context for those moments, no lens through which to view them other than my own experience, no perspective, just raw feelings of estrangement and alienation in a world where everyone else seemed to find their place.

After I became a psychiatrist I had access to every possible intervention. I tried most medications (always under another doctor's care) but none of them touched the Demon.

I also undertook many years of psychoanalysis, which I found helpful, but it didn't touch the Demon at all.

As a practising Episcopalian, I'd go to church every Sunday (more or less) but my religion didn't touch the Demon either. Pray as I might, and I'd pray every day, my prayers never stopped the Demon.

All that changed when I learned about the DMN and how to contain it. Now, with daily practice, I can fend off those attacks by redirecting my attention and those "episodes" have grown shorter and shorter.

The Demon no more

Of all the points I will make in this book, what I've told you about the Demon may be the most important. It's unlikely you'll read about it anywhere else because it's only recently that we have started to appreciate the full ramifications of the discovery of the TPN and DMN and how that knowledge can be applied in day-to-day life.

Not all of us who have ADHD contend with the Demon. If you're lucky enough to have escaped it, I'm happy for you. However, if you, like me, contend with the Demon, give redirecting your attention a try before you turn to medications or other more complicated interventions.

Keep in mind

~ The Demon is the unintended consequence of your imagination.

~ The Demon does not speak a truth it's received from above, or from anywhere else. It speaks only what it receives from you.

~ *You* are in charge of the Demon. Do not let it rule you.

~ Since you created it, you can shut it down as well.

~ Never forget, you create the Demon. Without you it doesn't exist.

Chapter 8

ADDICTION

In this chapter we will take a look at the close relationship between ADHD and what's usually called addiction. Just as my approach to ADHD in general is strength-based, so is my approach to the most dangerous habit that often accompanies ADHD, namely a reliance on drugs or maladaptive behaviours to achieve pleasure and relieve pain. This chapter will explore all of this and provides an action plan to escape the trap of addiction.

A seductive trap, not a moral failing

Addiction is a reliance on a means of gaining pleasure and reducing pain that does more harm than good yet is extremely difficult to give up. The word "addiction" – and especially the word "addict" – brings to mind no positive associations and a host of negative, shaming associations.

That's why I prefer to see addiction as a trap your genes and society have set for you. No one wants to fall into the trap, after all. If you reject the idea that addiction is a moral failing or a disease, you create a framework that allows for optimism and hope, both key elements in any effective plan to escape the trap.

The "trap model" also squares with reality. Most people who fall into the trap describe their first experience with whatever substance it happened to be as like finding at last the solution to life, discovering a way out of pain and into a life they could actually enjoy living. When that solution doesn't pan out, they find they are stuck, as if they had stumbled into quicksand. Treatment, therefore, is all about finding ways to get out of the quicksand, while also developing other ways to find joy and deal with pain.

Keep in mind

Willpower is great but compared to the power of genes and biology it's puny. Relying on willpower is like relying on a wish to make your dreams come true. Wishing is lovely but you need more concrete help to create change.

90% of people who have an addiction don't seek help

Keep in mind

It's a sad fact that each year 90 per cent of people who need substance use disorder (SUD) treatment don't seek professional help. There are many reasons for this but chief among them are:

~ shame and stigma, feeling afraid to tell anyone about the problem as it develops

~ not knowing what help is available or how effective it has become over the past decades

~ not knowing how or where to get the help that is needed

Finding pleasure and dealing with pain

Before we go any further, take some time to consider these two questions:

1 What do you do to relieve stress and pain?

2 How do you get pleasure in your life?

Knowing the answers to these questions is crucial. They can help you manage your ADHD and show you how to find pleasure and joy, its more reliable cousin, without danger.

When you are ready, turn the page and we'll consider some common ways people seek pleasure and relieve pain.

5 harmful ways to find pleasure (and deal with pain)

Let's take a look at some unhealthy methods you might use to manage your feelings and emotions.

~~~~~~~~~~~~~~~~~~~~~~~~~~~~~~~~

1. **Drugs and alcohol:** In my opinion, recreational drugs and alcohol pose the single most dangerous risk in life for people with ADHD. Addiction or substance use disorder (SUD) is 5–10 times more common in people who have ADHD than in the general population. Around 80 per cent begin using drugs and alcohol between the ages of 13 and 23, making those 10 years the major danger zone. Why is that window of time so dangerous? Well, most teenagers believe they'll live forever, which makes them ready, indeed eager, to take just about any risk, as long as it's exciting. When you add ADHD to the mix – remember, people with ADHD love risks because they are stimulating (see page 62) – you end up with young people who are ready to risk their lives in the name of adventure.

If you are a parent to a teenager with ADHD, here's some advice to prevent reliance on dangerous ways of finding pleasure and developing a substance use disorder in your children:

~ Educate – you can't explain the risks too often. It's a tricky business not to harangue them about it.

~ Model moderate behaviour around alcohol and other substances.

~ Role play what to do at parties when someone offers them drugs and alcohol.

~ Create a culture of honesty at home – you want your kids to feel safe to tell you the truth.

~ If an episode of excessive drinking or other drug-taking happens, be sure to react in a helpful way. Don't fly off the handle in anger or impose extreme punishments. **A word about punishments in ADHD: they don't work.**

2. **Behavioural addictions:** The most common of these are addictions to screens, food, shopping, exercise, gambling, and sex. These types of addictions used to be seen as a joke but they are no joke. The good news is that help is available and you can get it.

3. **Avoidance:** People with ADHD use avoidance as their primary defence against pain. They avoid things that might hurt them – such as learning a new skill, a new sport, or how to ask someone out on a date – even if those things might also be good for them.

4. **Isolation:** Withdrawing from other people is another common way of avoiding pain. We can send people away through both our words and our actions.

5. **Repellence:** Becoming as unappealing as you can possibly make yourself will keep people away. If no one wants to get close to you, no one can hurt you, right?

While life's pain can lead you into addiction or maladaptive patterns, it can save your life if you develop healthy methods for soothing pain and tapping into joy.

80% of addiction begins between the ages of 13 and 23

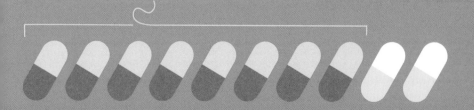

5 healthy ways to find pleasure (and deal with pain)

Now let's look at five effective and healthy methods you might use to manage your feelings and emotions.

~~~~~~~~~~~~~~~~~~~~~~~~~~~~~

1. **Connect with people:** This is by far the best method. Relationships are what make life good. Humans are social creatures. Every study ever undertaken on happiness rates relationships at the top. For a fact that seems so obvious it's amazing how many people live as if they don't know it. Recent research into human happiness found that human connection – love – is the most significant variable to predict lasting joy, fulfillment, and health over a lifetime. It's the best drug there is (see page 144).

2. **Physical exercise:** It's a proven fact that exercise boosts your mood, as well as making you think better. The only problem with exercise is getting yourself to do it in the first place. The best fix for that is to do it with someone else. Find a group exercise that you enjoy, whether walking, hiking, spinning, or dancing, and make a plan to go every week.

3. **Find a creative outlet:** People who have ADHD *need* creative outlets (see page 174). We need to express what's built up in our imaginations. If we don't have that outlet we get depressed. Most people, even experts in the field, don't know about this. That's because it hasn't made it into the "literature", as research is called, because it hasn't been studied. Nevertheless, I've studied it in myself my whole life, as well as in my patients. One reason why I write so many books is because I don't feel right if I don't have a book in progress. **One of the most effective suggestions I can make to my patients who have ADHD is to urge them to find a creative outlet.** Invariably, the ones who follow my advice see a quantum leap in their basic *joie de vivre*. Find a creative outlet that suits you – drawing, woodworking, knitting, or writing short stories – and do it regularly.

4. **Get enough sleep:** "Enough" sleep almost certainly means more sleep than you are getting right now. Our ADHD brains are so busy we *hate* to put aside all the stimulation and fall asleep. You may think of going to sleep as shutting down but your brain most definitely does not shut down while you are asleep. Not at all. First of all, there are dreams, right? Well, even more important than dreaming is the clean-up operation that swings into action while you sleep. A whole crew of your brain's finest neurons rolls up its sleeves and gets to work cleaning up the messes in your brain you made while you were awake. However, the cleaning crew can't get to work until your wakefulness centre shuts down, so sleep is essential. For advice about how to improve the quality of your sleep, see page 193.

5. **Get a dog:** OK, laugh if you want to but I'm serious. I know it's not a practical solution for everyone – some people can't do it because of space or allergies – and I also know how much it hurts when a beloved pet dies but, for my money, nothing beats a dog for pure, unadulterated, no-questions-asked love. Believe me, nothing creates joy in life more than love does. All you have to do is find love and cherish it. Dogs do that automatically for you. If you can't be a dog owner, visit a friend with a dog, or offer to walk a neighbour's dog, or look for a local dog-walking scheme.

Keeping these methods in mind and developing methods of your own will help you in your life, whatever your issues may be.

The reward deficiency syndrome

People with ADHD are born with their pleasure regulator set too low, which means that people who have ADHD must resort to extraordinary means to get ordinary pleasure. This is a hugely important point (one that most people have never heard of) so let me explain it some more.

Most people go through their days liking life – not loving it, necessarily, but glad to be alive. In fact, most people live each moment in a state of relative contentment, relative, that is, to being unhappy or upset about something.

They wake up in the morning and, like a thermostat being set where it should be, their mood is positive, not gleeful necessarily but pretty good.

In contrast, people with ADHD wake up in the morning the emotional equivalent of cold. In other words, their emotional thermostat is set quite low. They need to work to get happy. They need to make an effort to bring their pleasure setting up to where most people's is set automatically.

Tricks of the trade

"Ping" is my word for experiencing a brief moment of joy, such as hearing birdsong or sipping a fresh cup of coffee. We who have ADHD often let these moments pass unnoticed. One way to make them last is to take note of them by bursting into song – don't worry, no one will care – so hold on to the moment and remember it.

People with ADHD have to find ways every day to resurrect their mood, to elevate their emotional state from the doldrums to a state of satisfaction and joy. It's a daily chore because their resting state is set so low.

Kenneth Blum, a pharmacologist, developed this theory and named it the reward deficiency syndrome. It's based on a genetic difference in the dopamine D2 receptor. Blum actually developed a test you can take to see if you have that difference, and he also developed a treatment called precision addiction management (PAM) based on taking micronutrients. His theory explains the strong genetic component of all addictions/substance use disorders/compulsions.

The bottom line is we are not all born equal when it comes to dealing with dopamine (see page 134).

Dopamine: The magic molecule

Often called a "feel-good hormone", dopamine is a neurotransmitter that plays a primary role in the brain's reward system.

Essentially, our search for pleasure comes down to getting dopamine released into our synapses, the junctions between nerve cells in our brains. Each drop of dopamine creates the feeling we call pleasure. There are many roads to pleasure but all roads meet at "Dopamine Central", the final common pathway to pleasure.

The problems arise when we just can't get enough of that feeling of pleasure dopamine creates, always needing just one more hit. This is where addiction/ substance use disorder (SUD) begins. Addiction extends well beyond chemical substances to include a wide range of behaviours, from eating, shopping, screens, and exercise to gambling, danger-seeking, and sex, – any activity you'd like to cut back on but can't.

There are few topics in all of mental health as complex as the trap of not being able to give up a drug once you try it. A multitude of factors come into play, from your family history to how you were raised, to early exposure to substances, to the neighbourhood you live in, to the culture of the school you attended, to the presence or absence of trauma but a major star of the show is dopamine.

Here's one way to define this trap: any substance, activity, or relationship you'd like to cut back on but, despite genuine effort, can't.

Another definition is any substance, activity, or relationship that, when taken away so you can't access it, causes you to go into withdrawal, as defined by incessant cravings as well as physical signs like fever, elevated heart rate and blood pressure, rapid or shallow breathing, feelings of panic, physical agitation, itchiness, irritability, insomnia, and a general horrible feeling of sickness through and through, even wanting to die.

The cruel and devilish irony of this trap is that what begins in paradise ends up in hell.

What initially seemed like heaven, what appeared to open the door to happiness at last, what seemed to be the answer to all your prayers, your ticket out of the doldrums to a sweet life at last, all that dissolves in front of you and within you. In the most sadistic bait-and-switch ever known, the magic molecule, dopamine, loses its mojo. You're left with the physical need to keep using the substance, or keep doing whatever the activity was, or stay in the relationship, but now you get no reward. However, you have to keep doing it just to get relief from the pain withdrawal sets off.

So you see, *how* you get pleasure matters more than the pleasure itself. You must take care of your dopamine for it to take care of you.

Your action plan

Here's my seven-step plan to help you escape the trap.

1. Get a complete diagnosis

ADHD, when it occurs alongside addiction, usually comes with one or more other conditions as well. It's common for an anxiety disorder to appear in the mix, along with depression, perhaps a history of trauma or post-traumatic stress disorder (PTSD), as well as what's called rejection sensitive dysphoria, a condition in which a person over-reacts to the slightest perceived rejection or disappointment. Work with a professional to get an accurate and comprehensive diagnosis.

2. Develop a plan

Once you have a diagnosis you need to develop a plan. The best methods of getting out of the trap are also the least expensive and do not involve spending time in hospitals, retreats, ultra-expensive ranches, or other lavish institutions. It is better to stay as much in the world as you can while you figure out – with the help of a professional, chosen with care – other ways of finding pleasure and relieving pain than drugs or compulsive activities.

Keeping in mind the adaptive, healthy methods of finding pleasure and avoiding pain that you learned about earlier in the chapter, try building sleep, exercise, nutrition, meditation, and positive daily human moments of connection into your plan (see pages 142–161 and 184–203).

Keep in mind

Methods that do not work and should not form part of your plan are:

~ Tough love, which can be quite dangerous.

~ Lectures and exhortations to stop wasting and ruining your life.

~ Shaming and instilling guilt over the damage being done to family, friends, community, and concerned others.

~ The latest fad cure.

~ Stints in rehab with inadequate follow-up.

3. Seek empathy and optimism, reject shame and stigma

If you want to get out of the trap it is important to feel understood, not judged, to feel respected rather than scorned. There's a long list of things that might bring you joy and reduce your pain but they all begin with you feeling understood, valued, and optimistic. By far the best way to rid yourself of shame is to connect with someone who's been there, done that.

Meaningful education (the next step) can begin only after feelings of shame and stigma have been cleared and a tone of optimism sets in.

You need to know yourself before you can love yourself – you need to know just exactly who and what you're loving.

4. Educate yourself

You need to understand yourself. The more you understand what's going on within you and have that validated by another person or people, the more easily and quickly you can embrace those parts of yourself. Do I really mean you will embrace the ruinous habits you developed? Is it possible to embrace the person who developed them, the person who fell into the trap, namely, you? Yes, when you understand it, you will appreciate its positive contributions to who you are, not just the negative. This entire book is an exercise in learning how to embrace ADHD.

5. Find an ADHD coach or therapist who will oversee the entire process and meet with you regularly

This relationship will be the cornerstone of your treatment. This person will become your guide, your confidante, your go-to clinician come what may. They will organize and communicate with the other people involved in your treatment, such as a a psychologist if there's testing involved or a doctor if medication is to be used.

Your ADHD coach or therapist may handle helping you with improving executive function skills (see page 94) themselves or they may refer you to another coach designated to help you learn those skills.

Schedule regular follow-up visits with your treatment team, as often as the situation warrants. Success depends in large measure on the quality of the connection you establish with the team, especially the lead clinician who becomes your primary relationship in this ongoing effort.

Keep in mind

Almost everything that's good in life begins in connection, and almost everything that's not good begins in disconnection.

6. Address both the ADHD and the unhealthy ways you seek pleasure and manage pain simultaneously

Contrary to popular belief, it is fine, indeed indicated, to try stimulant medication. There's a good chance stimulant medication will help both the ADHD and the habits. See Chapter 13: Medication, pages 204–213) for more information about ADHD medication.

7. Medication-assisted treatment (MAT)

Twelve-step programmes like Alcoholics Anonymous and Narcotics Anonymous save lives but their success rate, if you define success as being sober after one year, is only 15 per cent. Now, however, with the advent of medication-assisted treatment (MAT), as well as family and community based treatments, the success rate has risen to around 70 per cent. The goal now is to bring more people into treatment. Your doctor can explain the range of medications available.

Tricks of the trade

Taking stimulant medication dramatically reduces the risk of addiction. Far from being gateway drugs, medications don't open the gate to abuse, they help to close it.

Finding freedom

My most important message is this: the power of human connection, combined with recent advances in science, can free you from the trap you fell into and restore you to health, better than ever. All you need is the right help. Make sure you work with professionals who are up on the science and exude intelligent optimism.

Informed love is the most potent therapy we have. When you are surrounded by a force field of informed, directed, and sustained positive energy, miracles become routine. Not only does recovery happen, but a person gets a second life, a second chance. Soon the things that seemed impossible beckon, well within reach.

Chapter 9

CONNECTION AND RELATIONSHIPS

Connection and its driving force – love – beat together as the heart of life. This topic is especially relevant to ADHD because most people with ADHD fumble with connections and love. I'm not just talking about romantic love, although that's definitely important. I'm talking about love of family, friendships, passionate interests, and hobbies, love of work, love of life – love of all kinds. Once you get love and give love, everything else follows. You've got it, as they say, made.

In this chapter, I will explain how connection serves as the foundation for everything in life that really matters, encourage you to make yourself vulnerable and open yourself up to love, and explore some of the common relationship issues for people with ADHD.

The power of human connection

Connection is the force that can make the biggest difference in a person's life. The most convincing evidence for this comes from the Harvard Study of Adult Development. The study began in 1938 with a cohort of male students, then expanded to include women and people from different socioeconomic strata, as well as the offspring of the participants.

Keep in mind

Human connection is the most powerful force for good in the world. Some people call it love.

The investigators tracked every imaginable variable in the subjects' lives and interviewed these people in person. It is the longest-running, most-comprehensive longitudinal study on happiness and wellbeing ever conducted.

When psychiatrist George Vaillant, a lead researcher, was asked what the study showed to be the most significant variable predicting lasting joy, fulfillment, and health over the course of a lifetime, his answer could not have been more succinct:

"Happiness is love. Full stop."

More than any other factor, the quality and depth of your relationships determine what kind of life you will lead. This is really good news because deep, loving connections are free and available to everyone – and if we manage them properly, they're a ton of fun (usually).

Am I telling you that the secret to a long and happy life is free, readily available, and fun? Yes. It is a proven fact. Prioritizing connection, nurturing connection every day in the details of life, is truly the best single step we can take to make life as good as it can be.

The perils of social isolation

Disconnection, on the other hand, kills. Loneliness and social isolation are as harmful as cigarette smoking or severe alcohol abuse. The Surgeon General of the United States named loneliness as the number one medical problem in the country. **Medical problem, not psychiatric problem.** And depression, which often stems from loneliness, is a leading cause of lost workdays as well as a complicating factor in many chronic conditions.

Furthermore, social isolation can kill you. The epidemiologist Lisa Berkman proved this decades ago in landmark studies that linked social isolation to early death. The studies showed that people with strong social ties were three times less likely to die early than those who were less connected to others. It was Berkman who showed that loneliness can be as bad for you as cigarette smoking, excessive use of alcohol, or not wearing a seatbelt in your car. It was such an unexpected finding that at first experts didn't believe the results. However, Berkman's findings have now been replicated in over a dozen studies around the world.

In fact, a 2015 study into loneliness and social isolation as risk factors for mortality found that loneliness is likely to increase your risk of early death by 26 per cent.

Loneliness is likely to increase your risk of early death by 26%

Finding your passion

Not long ago I was invited to give a talk to the student body at my old school. What many of the students at my old school – and at schools everywhere – hope to do, and what most of their parents also hope they will do, is gain admission to a top college or university. In my speech, however, I offered a completely different, far more sensible, and evidence-based point of view. I told the students that putting an extreme emphasis on getting into the "best" college led them away from the most important purpose of education, to fall in love.

I encouraged them to use their time at school to fall in love – with a subject, a book, a musical instrument, a dream, a philosophy. I explained that the importance of getting a top grade will fade over time; but falling in love with a topic, such as chemistry, can last a lifetime. If you fall in love, and deepen that love over time, you're set for life. The prestige of the college or university you attend doesn't matter one whit compared to the lifelong treasures that falling in love provides.

This is an important message for everyone. However, it's especially important for people who have ADHD because, typically, their grades will not gain them admission to the so-called top institutions, which often leaves them feeling second-rate. The good news is that in the long run it doesn't matter where you studied. What is important are the attitudes and skills you develop, and everyone can develop the attitudes and skills necessary for success and fulfilment.

What do I mean by love?

Love is the ultimate intensification of positive regard for a person, a place, an object, an idea, a mission, an activity, a hope, a dream, indeed for anything at all.

Love is the work of the imagination. Since imagination is the greatest asset we people with ADHD possess, we get a running start when it comes to love. In love, the imagination does its most creative work. Love looks at what most people call reality, imagines a better version, and then makes that version come to life.

I make a big deal of the L-word because I want to stress, unequivocally, how much it matters. Love matters more than anything else. You really shouldn't wait for it to happen. Go get love now. You can make it happen. How? By looking around.

Obstacles to love

Too many people hold back from love, especially people with ADHD.

They hold back from love out of fear, not wanting to appear foolish, needy, sappy, sentimental, or, even worse, unsophisticated or uncool. To combat this tendency, try saying to yourself, or writing on a note you attach to your bathroom mirror, "Don't hold back on life out of fear".

The best part of you wants to try, whatever the challenge might be. As long as you have support – again, the supreme importance of connection – you can handle any disappointment or setback. As the famous saying goes, "it is better to have loved and lost than never to have loved at all". You don't want to die regretting all the things you never did. You don't want your last words to be, "If only...".

Keep in mind

You miss 100 per cent of the shots you don't take.

Opening yourself up to love of all kinds

If you have ADHD, it's likely you spent a good bit of your growing-up years putting up walls around you, learning how to conceal or even shut down your true self in order to avoid the judgements, jeers, and rejections of the outside world.

Over time, you built a suit of armour that served you well. Now, however, that armour is making it difficult for people to get to know you, let alone love you. And it is also getting in your way when you want to love someone yourself. Imagine what it would be like to kiss – or be kissed by – someone wearing a full suit of armour. It's not a pretty picture.

To find love you need to make yourself vulnerable. You need to remove your armour and open yourself up to the world. You need to open yourself up to friendships, romance, passionate interests, not to mention love of the person you treat worst and seem to love least: yourself.

Over time, your loves can make up the most beautiful garden imaginable. A garden full of all the many connections you hold dear, each one of them unique and deserving of attention. Those connections might comprise all kinds of love – love of a person or two; love of a dog (I hope!) or any animal, even a stuffed one; love of nature; love of ideas; love of whatever art appeals to you; love of a mathematical proof; love of riding a bicycle, or repairing one, or inventing a new one. You get the idea.

There are infinite ways to give and receive love. I'm hoping you will give love a chance.

Finding the right partner

If you want to be happy in life, you need to find the right person, whether that is a long-term partner or spouse. This is especially important for people with ADHD because of how often they can get this critical choice wrong.

Finding the right partner means finding someone you love who loves you back. That's obvious, right? Yet it's amazing how many people don't do that, especially people who have ADHD.

One common, maladaptive pattern for people with ADHD is to fall for someone who has the potential to be critical, reprimanding, controlling, and punitive. Why fall for such a person? Because someone who has ADHD can easily get the idea that that's what they need in order to do well. No one ever told them that they're lovable as they are or that they don't need to be made over or controlled.

Another common, maladaptive pattern is for the person who has ADHD to fall for someone whose life is a bit of a disaster. Why? Because people who have messy lives are stimulating, and those of us with ADHD crave high stimulation. And on top of that, we are born rescuers (see page 61). We relish the opportunity to save someone.

Obviously, it's much better to fall for someone who loves you for who you are, someone who doesn't want to change you, someone who is stable but not boring. If you have a tendency to fall into one of these destructive patterns, consult an expert in order to learn about and then break the habit.

Practical solutions to relationship obstacles

Let's take a look at some common ways that couples who have ADHD (in one or both members of the couple) get into trouble and I'll offer some tips on how to solve those issues.

Keep in mind

True connection begins in an accurate understanding of the other person's reality.

Feeling misunderstood

Feeling misunderstood may be the number one complaint in life with ADHD. The partner who has ADHD may lament, "You just don't understand me." Frequently, when ADHD is in the mix, that statement is correct. If you feel completely misunderstood, your relationship is bound to be doomed.

To save the relationship, both partners need to take the matter seriously. Each member of the couple should clearly explain to the other who they are and what their internal reality is all about. These explanations need to be clear enough for the partners to understand the other's internal reality and also to recognize how much it differs from their own internal reality.

Mistakes

When one member of a couple doesn't understand ADHD it can lead to them blaming or berating the person who has ADHD for their forgetfulness, lateness, and other instances of poor executive functioning (see page 70), not realizing that they can't help it. One solution is to recognize the inadvertent and unintentional nature of the mistakes. After all, ADHD is rooted in neurology, not in psychology. This knowledge can save relationships.

ADHD is never an excuse for not taking responsibility but it is a powerful explanation. Once the person without ADHD understands that their partner doesn't make mistakes on purpose – isn't late on purpose, doesn't forget birthdays on purpose, doesn't fail to complete tasks on purpose – it is possible for them to stop taking the missteps personally, which makes it easier for them to forgive and move on.

Yes, the underlying problems still need to be fixed. However, when the partner without ADHD stops taking all the mistakes personally, the couple can work as a partnership, rather than as adversaries, to solve the problems and come up with creative solutions.

Arguments and misunderstandings

When it comes to communication, there can often be an enormous difference between the intention behind a remark and its impact. People who have ADHD are especially prone to overlook the impact of what they have said or done, as long as their intent was positive.

Rather than getting defensive and telling your partner that they have no right to be upset if the impact was wildly at odds from the intention, it's better to recognize the legitimacy of their feelings, and then explain how different your intention was from the impact of your words. This is not hairsplitting. Separating intention from impact can prevent prolonged, bitter arguments and save relationships from fatal misunderstandings.

Dishonesty

Another common relationship issue is dishonest engagement. When people with ADHD feel trapped, our first response can be to panic and lie, even though we know the truth will come out.

If you fall into this trap, try to avoid compounding the problem with an insincere apology or a patronizing expression like the famous "I'm sorry you feel that way", which only throws fuel on the fire. It's likely a partner will want you to empathize more. "You're sorry I feel this way? Well, what about *why* I feel this way?" Instead, own the problem and tell your partner you're going to work on breaking the habit of lying. Explain that your lies are not malicious, just born out of desperation, and you understand that this is no excuse for your behaviour. Hopefully, this will help your partner not to think of you in such a negative light.

Blame and being in the right

People with ADHD have a terrible tendency to externalize blame. (We will blame the door when we stub our toe on it!) Is "I'm sorry, but..." one of your familiar refrains? The "but" is what kills you. You messed up. Just own it.

Another important point is how little being right matters in a relationship. The goal is for the pair of you to get along, not to establish who was right. The two are often mutually exclusive. It is better to say "I was wrong" without believing it than to establish that you were right and lose your partner for the foreseeable future.

Not listening

"Stop nodding at me. I know you're not even hearing what I'm saying." This is a phenomenon I call the ADHD nod. We use it to get people off our backs. If the other person doesn't know us well, they'll fall for it. But if they're our partner, then they will recognize it right away for the brush-off it is.

When you get caught, don't deny it. Just say, "Sorry, would you mind running that by me again?" And don't get defensive if they say, "Don't give me that sorry routine, I'm fed up with you not listening." Instead, validate their reaction. "Yes, I know. This ADHD thing can be such a drag. I get frustrated myself by how my mind just wanders off. I try to control it but my mind has a mind of its own."

Take a risk

For this book to do for you what it can, I'm hoping you will take what may feel like a colossal risk – though in fact it is no risk at all – and open yourself up to love and connection in all its guises. Connection is the foundation upon which everything that matters in life gets built. Nurture your garden of connections and your life will flourish.

Once you get love and give love, everything else follows.

The real risk lies in doing nothing.

Chapter 10

CREATIVITY

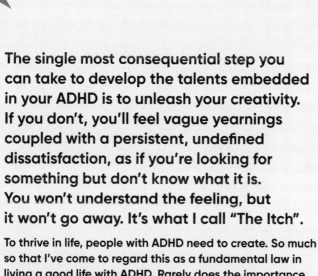

The single most consequential step you can take to develop the talents embedded in your ADHD is to unleash your creativity. If you don't, you'll feel vague yearnings coupled with a persistent, undefined dissatisfaction, as if you're looking for something but don't know what it is. You won't understand the feeling, but it won't go away. It's what I call "The Itch".

To thrive in life, people with ADHD need to create. So much so that I've come to regard this as a fundamental law in living a good life with ADHD. Rarely does the importance of the regular exercise of creativity get mentioned as a means of making the best out of life with ADHD. But it should. Because it works like nothing else, with the possible exception of ongoing love.

"The Itch"

People with ADHD are born with a unique trait that I call "The Itch". Although you won't find discussion of the Itch in the DSM, it is likely you will recognize its presence in life with ADHD.

The Itch is a trait you are born with. It is an irritant, an unpleasant feeling you want to relieve as soon as possible, just like a regular itch. However, unlike a regular itch, which can be alleviated with a good scratch, the Itch can only be assuaged through behaviours. A major factor in separating good outcomes in ADHD from bad outcomes is the method a person finds to scratch the Itch.

What I am calling the Itch is recognized in other contexts by other names. Creative people, for example, often locate it outside of themselves and call it their "muse" or "inspiration". I believe the Itch, that feeling of basic irritation or dissatisfaction, is what drives creativity in people with ADHD.

The Itch is like the grain of sand in an oyster that begets a pearl; it's an irritation that can lead to beauty. However, it can also get those of us who have ADHD into a lot of trouble.

The danger of the Itch

It's deeply ironic that the Itch, which can lead to our greatest moments of creativity and originality, can also trigger our demise. Just as ordinary life spurs us on to improve it by building or creating something, it can also tempt us to alter our internal reality through certain behaviours, such as casual sex or gambling or by means of substances like alcohol or other drugs. As I pointed out in Chapter 8: Addiction (see pages 122–141), it is far more common to fall into that trap if you have ADHD than if you don't. That's because you're ready to try anything, including doing some really bad things, to scratch the Itch.

To tackle the negative aspects of the Itch, my advice is to engage with the 10-step plan in Chapter 4: A Basic Plan to Live Your Best Life (see pages 66–79).

Recognizing your innate creativity

What is creativity, but impulsivity gone right? And impulsivity is one of the three symptoms that defines ADHD, according to the DSM, so those of us with ADHD have it in spades.

People generally regard impulsivity as a nuisance rather than a gift. What they don't appreciate is that when you release control, which you do when an impulse interrupts you, you open the gates to the new.

Original ideas arrive unplanned. It is as if they appear out of nowhere, a sneak attack from the unconscious upon consciousness. For that reason, just as I said in Chapter 1: What is ADHD? (see page 24), while we do want to strengthen the brakes on the ADHD brain – that brain with a Ferrari engine but only bicycle brakes – we don't want to strengthen them so much that they block out the valuable moments of impulse we deem creative.

Keep in mind

I learned a good definition of creativity from my maths teacher in the eleventh grade. "Be creative," he'd say, when advising us how to use our creativity to solve a maths problem we'd never seen before. Then he added something I remember to this day, 58 years later. "Creativity is the recombination of the elements of your experience into new forms."

And here is my own definition, based on my experience as a writer:

Creativity is the ability to allow your unconscious unfiltered access to your conscious mind.

The creative process

I encouraged you to sing when you ping in Chapter 8 (see page 132). I mention this because it provides an example from my own life of my allowing my unconscious access to my writing.

The word "ping" was nowhere in my plans for this book, nor had I ever used the word before. It broke into my mind, unbidden, during the writing process, and when it did it arrived as part of the sentence, "Sing when you ping!" That's the unconscious in action.

Creativity is the most valuable gift we who have ADHD possess. Other people create too, of course, but we do it as a way of life. We're forever at it in our minds. Sometimes we wish we could shut it off. It's ironic that what we do best is something we can't do on demand or explain to others how it's done. We just do it.

Most of us do what we do because we can't not do it. Although imagination stands out as the most valuable and defining characteristic of ADHD, it can also feel like a curse at times. In the hands of the DMN (the Default Mode Network, see page 110) or when the Itch leads us astray, we can torture ourselves, lose perspective, and roam the dark forest of doom and gloom alone. That's why it's so important to learn how to control the DMN or scratch the Itch, lest you abandon your use of creativity altogether and turn to numbing your mind.

To sing when you ping, to use your creativity well and develop it over the course of your lifetime, especially if you have ADHD, it's a good idea to know how much you don't know and to accept how much you depend upon your unconscious.

Trust your unconscious

What's the secret of creativity? You could ask a hundred people that question and get a hundred different answers. From me you'll get answer number 101: trust your unconscious.

Trusting your unconscious means opening yourself up to it, not rejecting anything new as unacceptable or too "out there". Remember, many new ideas get ridiculed at first. Allow your unconscious to show you its ideas before you reject them out of hand.

Trusting your unconscious also means relinquishing control. People with ADHD often cling to control like a life raft because they fear they'll drown in life's details if they let go of control. In fact, often, by letting go of control, by

developing your negative capability, you can enter into a whole new world, your world of originality and vision, a world created by your unconscious. By unbinding yourself from the chains of control you allow yourself access to the special chamber of your imagination that your unconscious furnishes and decorates. It's where you'll find your unique treasures, if you'll allow yourself the freedom to do so.

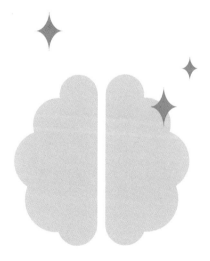

What if I'm not creative?

My first response to this question is to ask you if you're a worrier. Almost everyone who has ADHD is a worrier. If you want to see proof of how creative you are, just look at your worries. Not only do you have to be super creative to come up with all those worries, you also have to be proficient at suspending disbelief, because many of the things you worry about are beyond belief.

If you're not convinced that you're creative, I suggest you try one of the following exercises:

~ **Automatic writing.** Take a piece of paper or open up your laptop and just start writing words, any words. Don't stop. Sense is not required. Spelling be damned. Just keep writing for three minutes. The results may seem weird and nonsensical but you might find that your unconscious reveals an idea, an image, or a project you want to develop. Do this a few times and you will quickly discover you're more creative than you thought.

~ **Sit down at a piano and write a song.** You don't need any musical training to do this. Just let your fingers play over the keys. In a few tries, you will have composed a simple melody. You will find the music in you that you never knew was there.

~ **Draw something.** Just put your pencil, pen, or charcoal on the paper and let your unconscious rip. Usually we take such good care to be in control (to be appropriate, polite, and well-organized) that we stifle the creator within us. This puts the total kibosh on someone who has ADHD. It's not good for anyone, but for those of us with ADHD it's like cancelling out our imaginations. So let go of control if you can and just draw.

~ **Keep a dream journal.** Do you want evidence of your creativity? Look no further than your dreams. Assuming you're able to recall your dreams, keep a pen and journal next to your bed and write down a quick description of what you dreamed as soon as you wake up. In fact, you'll be activating your unconscious simply by paying attention to it consciously.

~ **Arrange flowers.** Go to your local flower market, florist, or shop that sells fresh flowers and buy several bunches. Take them home and try your hand at floral arrangement.

~ **Take photographs.** Spend an afternoon taking pictures. Try shooting them for their creative value, rather than just recording images of people and places you want to remember. Be an artist with your camera.

~ **Write a review.** Go to a movie, play, or sports game and then write an account of it that you think would be of interest to a reader.

~ **Cook something new.** Go into your kitchen and give yourself one hour to cook something you've never cooked before, using only the ingredients you have on hand. Remember, you're not going to be graded on this. It's purely to see if this exercise arouses a dormant chef within you.

~ **Fantasize.** Sit down in a comfortable chair in a peaceful place and fantasize about anything. This is not meditation, which is all about detaching from your thoughts. This is active fantasizing. Assign yourself a topic or throw caution to the wind and see where your mind wanders. Once it seizes upon something, whether it be imagining your dream house or conjuring up the plot of a novel you'd like to write, try not to let it go. This is the heart of the creative process. One of the muscles creative people need to build is the muscle of sustainability.

Finding your creative outlet

You need to find and develop an activity that really taps into your imagination. If you engage in that activity regularly – every day if you can – I guarantee you'll be amazed by the outcome.

The important thing is to stick at it for more than just a few days. The good news is you will want to stick at it if you pick the right outlet.

Your creative outlet can be anything you like to do, as long as it allows your imagination to roam free. It could be cooking, or starting your own business, or composing music, or dancing, or building a shed from scratch in your garden, or writing a series of sonnets, to name just a few options. Create in whatever medium feels right to you. It doesn't matter what outlet you choose. What matters is that you find it and develop it.

To really satisfy the Itch, your creative outlet must meet two requirements:

~ It must be challenging – if it's not, you'll get bored, and people with ADHD can't tolerate boredom.

~ It must excite you and turn you on. In other words, it must be "right" for you.

If you put those two requirements together, you have what I call your "right difficult".

Finding your right difficult is almost as crucial as falling in love with the right person. Almost. Finding your right difficult is huge, because once you find it, you'll be using it, doing it, cursing it, loving it, hating it, and living under its spell for the rest of your life.

Take pride

Creativity developed by the pursuit of the "right difficult" cooks up the best ADHD you'll ever have. And that's where you want to be. You want to be in the zone, on your game, not looking at what everyone else is doing but wrapped up in what you've got going on.

So there you have it. My game plan to recognize, define, use, and develop creativity, combined with my call to the ADHD World to rise up in unison and sing. Be full of joy for who you are, for all you represent, for all you, and your brothers and sisters, bring to this world.

Chapter 11

CAREERS

Arthur C. Brooks, a social scientist and columnist at *The Atlantic*, says, "What matters is not so much the 'what' of a job but more the 'who' and the 'why': Job satisfaction comes from people, values, and a sense of accomplishment." This is especially important for people with ADHD because we tend to be mission-driven far more than leader-driven.

The more we feel a part of something larger than ourselves – the more connected we feel to the values and purpose of the company we work for – the greater our satisfaction will be, which in turns raises and sustains our motivation to work as hard and creatively as we can.

However, job satisfaction is not entirely due to external factors. A study of genetically identical twins who were adopted separately and raised apart, thereby creating a lifelong nature vs nurture experiment, attributed 30 per cent of job satisfaction to genetic factors.

The right job, not just any job

When it comes to finding the right job, the biggest mistake I see people with ADHD make is to spend too much time trying to get good at what they're bad at. By setting a determined course in precisely the wrong direction, they take one of their chief strengths – determination – and turn it into a liability. In a valiant attempt to fill a gap in their self-esteem, they take on jobs at which they're bound to fail. In so doing, they can waste time, sometimes years, banging their heads against a brick wall, trying to get good at a job that doesn't suit them.

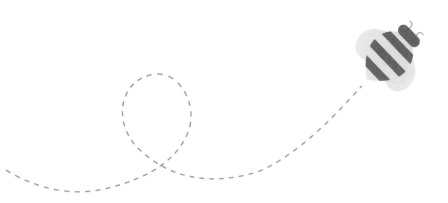

In the summer of 1969, I took a job selling encyclopedias door-to-door and discovered first-hand the wisdom of not spending too much time trying to get good at something you're bad at. Not only was I bad at selling encyclopedias, I was monumentally terrible. I couldn't understand why I couldn't do what the others in my team could. After six weeks, I hadn't made a single sale. At that point, I faced a decision that most people with ADHD face early in their careers: keep trying or get out. Even though I desperately wanted to keep at it, to make some sales, I knew it was never going to happen. So I got out.

My advice is to find the *right* job, not just any job. Find a good fit. Don't waste years trying to get good at what you're bad at. The right job lies at the intersection of two overlapping sets: the set of everything you're really good at doing and the set of everything you really like to do. In the space where those two sets overlap, is where you ought spend as much of your time as you can; it's where you should look for your ideal career.

Career

Things you really like to do

Things you're really good at

Four steps to the ideal job

Arthur C. Brooks, who tackles questions of meaning and happiness in his "How to Build a Life" column for *The Atlantic*, suggests four elements necessary for the ideal job:

1 **The work must be the reward.** In my vocabulary, that's the equivalent of stating that the work should be play.

2 **Interesting is better than fun.** This is in keeping with an ADHD person's primary need for stimulation and engagement.

3 **The path of the best career is rarely a straight line.** That is especially true of people who have ADHD. Our route is circuitous indeed.

4 **The passion you feel for the job must be harmonious not obsessive.** This is what I call finding your "right difficult" (see page 174).

The importance of play

I recommend that people who have ADHD find work that's basically play.

You probably think you know what I mean by the word "play", but I bet you don't. I'm not advising you to become a free spirit and go wherever the wind takes you. I'm not advising you to spend your life doing what school children do at breaktime (although you'd be surprised how useful that time turns out to be). No. What I'm asking you to do is remember what it was like when you were a child and to retrieve the most important skill you perfected in childhood, the skill to play.

My definition of "play" is any activity that lights up your imagination. Any activity in which you become creatively engaged.

The opposite of play is doing exactly what you're told. The world no longer needs people who do nothing more than exactly what they're told. What the world needs now, more than ever, is humans who do what their brains are uniquely equipped to do: think, innovate, create, envision, dream.

Never stop being playful

I learned about the importance of imagination in a work context when I did some consultation work for the chemistry department of a high-ranking university 20 years ago. Every year the department accepted some of the most gifted graduate and post-doctoral students from around the world. And every autumn, in response to the mandate, "Go into the lab and discover new knowledge", the new students divided into one of two groups:

~ One group would freeze up. They would promise to work all hours and gladly do any task but they couldn't come up with a question they wanted to answer on their own.

~ The other group would race into the lab, eager to use all the department's resources to investigate the questions they'd been thinking about for years.

The first group, who had worked hard at school to do exactly what they were told to do, had let their ability to play atrophy. The second group had never lost its ability to play, which meant they were ready to apply their imaginations full force.

Be true to yourself, without fear

As you learned in Chapter 10: Creativity (see pages 162–175), imagination is one of ADHD's greatest assets, but it can also become our worst enemy if we don't learn how to control the DMN (see page 110). However, once we are able to control the DMN, we are poised perfectly to play, to invent, to create, to discover.

Perhaps you don't consider your imagination to be a special gift. Perhaps you take it for granted since you've always had it. But look around.

Look at all the people who never have new ideas, who look at you cross-eyed when you introduce one, who fear and even attack new ideas. You need to understand just how different you are – in a good way – if you are to deal successfully with all the people who lack imagination.

Whatever the job you choose, be sure you play as much as you can every day. In play you're at your best. You do your most important work in play.

Keep in mind

An ideal career is some form of play that you get paid to do.

Chapter 12

HEALTH AND WELLBEING

"Not now, maybe later" is how a lot of people who have ADHD react when someone brings up exercise, lifestyle changes, or anything else that reminds them of the things they know they should be doing but haven't got around to actually doing.

Those of us with ADHD notoriously neglect the basics of self-care because it's boring! It's the same reason we so often neglect the household basics, such as paying bills or doing the laundry. Boring is our kryptonite.

In this chapter, I'm going to urge you to get healthy and explain why that is so important. But the last thing I want to do is motivate you through guilt. Instead, the programme I'm recommending is designed to be taken at your own pace and elicit your enthusiastic, guilt-free participation.

Why your health matters

The need to live a healthy lifestyle is rooted in rock-solid science. According to the World Health Organization (WHO), 61 per cent of all deaths are directly linked to chronic, preventable, lifestyle-related diseases, such as heart disease, adult-onset diabetes, obesity, stroke, metabolic syndrome, COPD (chronic obstructive pulmonary disease), and various forms of cancer. The two leading causes of preventable deaths, smoking and obesity, are rooted in unhealthy lifestyles.

Although most of us are aware that unhealthy living has an impact on our longevity, many of us choose to focus on the now, adopting an attitude of "It won't happen to me". But it does happen to us. If you take action now, you will increase your chances of living a lot longer. It is not too late. But you can't keep putting it off.

If everyone made just four adjustments to their lifestyle, those alarming WHO numbers would change dramatically. Which four?

Keep in mind

People with ADHD are inveterate procrastinators. Don't put off making lifestyle changes that will improve your health, and possibly your longevity too. Act now.

1 Get as close as you can to your ideal weight.

2 Follow a healthy diet.

3 Get regular exercise.

4 Don't smoke.

Unfortunately, many of us who have ADHD ignore these simple rules. It's not because we don't care. We do care. The problem for us is that getting into a healthy lifestyle requires planning, consistency, commitment, the delaying of gratification, attention to boring details, and daily follow-through, none of which people with ADHD are very good at.

61% of all premature deaths are linked to preventable, lifestyle-related diseases

It begins with your attitude

The main reason people find making lifestyle changes so difficult is their negative attitude. Do you recognize these excuses?

"I don't have enough discipline."

"I can't do it."

"Every time I try, I fail."

Don't let that negative inner voice put you off. Why? Because this time you will succeed. Yes, I said succeed. There is absolutely no reason for you not to, other than your not trying. It may sound hokey, but this is now a proven fact:

Whether you think you can or you think you can't, you're right.

As artificial and contrived as it may sound, if you start today to tackle life with a can-do, rather than a can't-do, attitude, you will discover the magic in can-do. You don't even have to deep down believe it. You'd be dishonest if you said right from the start, "OK, sure, I believe." Of course you'll start off with doubts. But don't lead with them. Lead with whatever positivity you can muster. **Speak the words out loud, even if you feel like you're lying through your teeth, it helps make them come true. Try it. You'll see.**

To do this you will need to come up with your own script, words that truly come from you. To help you get started, here's a few examples:

"Go away, you negative voices. I'm done with you."

"Today I'm going to nail it."

"I won't hold back on life out of fear ever again."

"Hello, self. You know what? I really like you!"

"Guess what? I really am a good person!"

Speak your can-do script out loud every day, as often as you can. It's your way of coming out of hiding, of saying, "Watch out world, here I come!" I'm telling you, this works for a lot of people. If you give it a chance it could work for you too.

Once you silence your negativity and put yourself on the side of can-do, you're ready to start living healthily. Why? Because you'll want to. It's that easy.

Lifestyle factors that promote good health

When it comes to creating a healthier lifestyle, there are four key elements you can easily and immediately adjust to optimize health, both physical and mental.

2 Physical exercise

3 Nutrition

1 Sleep

4 Meditation, mindfulness, and breathwork

I call these the "Fab Four".

In fact, there's also a fifth ingredient necessary for a good life: love. Love is incredibly important for a healthy, happy life. I don't just mean romantic love. I mean the entire spectrum of positive connections in life. The more time you spend in positive and loving states of mind, the healthier and happier you'll be. However, I've already devoted a whole chapter to connection (see Chapter 9, pages 142–161), so in this chapter I'm going to concentrate on the Fab Four.

Keep in mind

Physical and mental health are joined at the hip. It's almost impossible to have one without the other. In fact, in his book *Brain Energy*, Harvard psychiatrist Christopher Palmer makes a strong case that one of the best ways to cure or prevent a mental disorder is to lead a healthy lifestyle, and that most mental disorders have a root cause in unhealthy ways of living.

Sleep

I put sleep first because it is the factor most often ignored by people who have ADHD. Our super-active brains can be difficult to shut down, which makes it hard to fall asleep. And once we are asleep, the opposite problem arises, namely, we don't arise – once we're down, we're down.

There are a whole host of benefits linked to getting the sleep you need. A partial list includes:

~ **increased mental acuity**

~ **marked reduction** in the risk of depression

~ **marked reduction** in developing high blood pressure

~ **greater emotional control**

~ **reduction in incidence** of viral infections due to the boost in immune function sleep provides

~ **sustained feelings** of vitality and zest

So, if you get the sleep you need then all your dreams will come true? Well, maybe not, but you stand a much better shot at fulfilling your dreams if you get enough sleep!

After hearing thousands of stories of sleep problems from my patients who have ADHD, I've learned that each solution must be tailored to the individual patient. However, there are certain commonalities that have led me to create the following sleep prescription, specifically designed for people who have ADHD.

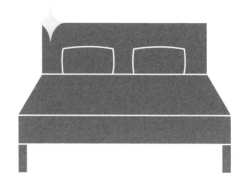

How to get a good night's sleep

~ **Get psyched to sleep!** Treat getting to sleep like it's the single most important thing you do for yourself every day, which it is! Give it the enthusiasm and priority it deserves. Most adults need around eight hours of sleep a night. Some lucky few need much less, and some unlucky few need much more. A simple rule is you need as much sleep as it takes for you to wake up without an alarm clock.

~ **Embrace sleep gently.** We people who have ADHD usually jump into things. We leap! We dive! We claw and scratch until we achieve our goal! That attitude is not the way to approach getting to sleep. Instead, think of sleep as a loving spirit who's inviting you to take a journey through the night into an enchanted kingdom called Dreamland. Let it guide you, gently, slowly toward sleep. The trick is to let go, which is best done gradually.

~ **Don't sleep holding your phone.** Using your phone close to bedtime can affect your sleep. To ensure an undisturbed night's sleep, keep you phone on your bedside table. Better still, leave it in another room, along with devices such as tablets and laptops.

~ **Don't drink alcohol before you go to bed.** If you have a glass of wine with dinner, leave it at that. Sure, alcohol makes you sleepy in the short run. But in the long run it impairs your sleep, which means the sleep you get is not nearly as restorative as it should be.

~ **Train yourself.** Develop a bedtime and a getting-up time. If you stick to that routine, going to sleep and waking up at the same times each day, your brain and body rhythms will get in sync, helping your brain to anticipate and naturally start to shut down at bedtime.

Physical exercise

You may be surprised to learn that the mental health benefits of exercise equal, if not surpass, the cardiovascular benefits. Among the many benefits that exercise provides to the brain, a few of the leading ones include:

~ **reduced anxiety** – regular exercise is a superb anti-anxiety agent

~ **reduced depression** – I recommend trying exercise before you try taking antidepressants

~ **enhanced concentration and memory,** which is especially helpful in ADHD

~ **increased levels of epinephrine, norepinephrine, and dopamine,** the same neurochemicals that are often used to treat ADHD (see page 208)

~ **proliferation of synapses,** the junctions between neurons, or nerve cells, in the brain, a hugely important factor in promoting memory and cognitive acuity

~ **production of an array of peptides, hormones, coenzymes,** and other molecules the brain loves

Stimulate your cerebellum

In addition to regular fitness routines, there's a specific type of exercise that is particularly helpful for ADHD. Recent research has shown a link between the cerebellum, a part of the brain located at the back of the head, and the frontal lobes, the place in the brain where all the action is in ADHD. We've known for years that the cerebellum controls balance, but it is only recently that we've learned that the cerebellum is intimately involved in frontal lobe functions like planning and organizing, as well as regulating emotion, all tasks that can be problematic in ADHD.

If you stimulate the cerebellum by doing regular physical exercises that challenge balance, such as standing on one leg or sitting on an exercise ball with your feet off the floor, you will see marked improvement in the symptoms of ADHD.

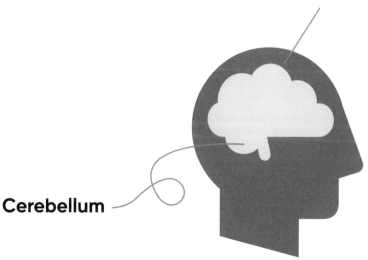

Frontal lobe

Cerebellum

Nutrition

The greatest danger for people with ADHD lies in eating what they shouldn't. Since carbs promote dopamine (that magic molecule we met in Chapter 8, see page 134), it's easy for someone with ADHD to self-medicate with carbs and sugar.

So what should we eat? You'll find lots and lots of advice about healthy eating in books, magazines, and online. Here are a few tips to help you on your way:

~ **Make healthy choices.** As much as possible, stick with wholefoods. The closer you can get to a vegan diet, the better.

~ **Try going gluten-free and dairy-free.** I've had patients resolve all the negative symptoms of ADHD just by taking those two steps.

~ **Don't forget to eat.** People with ADHD can become so wrapped up in what they are doing that they skip meals inadvertently. If that's an issue for you, try setting alarms or reminders for meal times.

~ **Hydrate!** Drink lots of water. No, you don't need to drink 4 litres (7 pints) of water a day or whatever the latest craze may be, but your body loves you to keep the water coming. Just don't make it sugar water, such as soft drinks and fruit juices, or caffeinated drinks.

~ **Use food as a catalyst of connection.** Use meals to bring people together and get their Vitamin Connect (see page 201). And by all means, serve wine with your food. Just let moderation be your guide. Wine is so wonderful, you want to learn to drink in moderation so you never have to give it up.

Meditation, mindfulness, and breathwork

The reason meditation and mindfulness get so much good publicity is because they work. Just how they work is up for grabs, but the fact they work is beyond question. It is possible that mindfulness meditation subdues or deactivates the Default Mode Network (DMN, see page 110), which means mindfulness training can be a godsend for people with ADHD.

The impact of mindfulness training has been studied in depth during the opening decades of the twenty-first century. Due to the pioneering work of psychiatrists Lidia Zylowska and Susan Smalley, as well as studies by many other psychiatrists, mindfulness training is now established as a treatment for ADHD with a success rate on a par with medication. One of the first studies showed that an eight-week programme in mindfulness training led to significant improvement in inattentive ADHD as well as emotional control on a par with results from medication. Numerous other studies have replicated those results.

There are lots of user-friendly meditation and mindfulness apps available that can help you get started. It's worth trying one of them.

Alternatively, try doing some breathing exercises. I find they suit me better than regular meditation. On the next page you'll find a breathwork routine I use whenever I want to hit my reset button. By focussing on my breathing I can deny admittance to the myriad other thoughts that are trying to get into my mind.

A simple breathing exercise

~ **Sit in a chair,** with your feet on the floor and your arms and hands on the arms of the chair.

~ **Close your eyes** and focus on your breathing.

~ **Take a deep breath in** to the count of eight.

~ **Hold your breath** for six counts.

~ **Breathe out slowly** for ten counts.

~ **Hold your breath** for six counts.

~ **Continuing to focus on your breathing,** repeat the sequence five more times.

Create a plan that's just right for you

You don't have to be a gym rat or a natural athlete to get into a regular exercise programme, and you don't have to have a PhD in chemistry to eat right. What you need to do is find a solution that works for you.

You'd be surprised how easy it can be to get the exercise you need. For example, one of my patients got talking to a friend about how much they wished they could get more exercise. Using the ingenuity of their ADHD, they asked around their neighbourhood and found three like-minded women.

Now five women take 30-minute walks together three mornings a week. Not only do they all get the exercise they need, they also get a big dose of Vitamin Connect.

Another patient of mine, a 45-year-old call-centre supervisor, knew he needed more exercise but he had to overcome two obstacles: he couldn't leave the office during the working day and he hated going to the gym. So he brought the gym to him. He actually likes those resistance bands you can stretch against, and he loves to dance, so three times a week he secludes himself in his office for 15 minutes. First he uses the bands to work out, then he puts on his headphones and dances, giving himself a workout that he actually enjoys and wants to do.

Think about what's really stopping you from making healthy changes to your life and then use your super-creative ADHD brain to come up with a plan, however eccentric, that really suits you.

Find your motivation

Once you have a plan, you need the energy and motivation to follow it. You may doubt you have the motivation but you wouldn't be reading this book if you weren't at least somewhat motivated to change. So let that side of yourself take the lead.

What you think of as a lack of motivation is really the lack of a plan and someone – a friend, partner, boss, coach, or mentor – to cheer you on. Cheerleaders for adults? You bet! They're worth their weight in gold. Lots of people pretend they don't need or want someone to cheer them on, but almost all of us do.

Don't tell me – and definitely don't tell yourself – that you're too lazy. It's time for you to side with the part of you that knows you're not.

Keep in mind

You already have all the motivation you need – everyone does, especially people with ADHD – you just haven't tapped into it yet.

Don't try to do it alone

It's a lot easier to sustain motivation if you have someone to work with you. Energy increases exponentially when you team up with a person or with a group.

Team up with a friend to exercise together and encourage each other or look for someone who's experienced in coaching people who have ADHD. (All you need to do is search online for "ADHD coaches".)

Working with a coach or a friend, you can outline your goals and then draw up a schedule for working toward those goals. Having a schedule as well as accountability may feel intimidating at first, but you'll soon find that those factors motivate and sustain you. The secret is teamwork and accountability.

Keep in mind

Put together a team you know you can work with enthusiastically. Your chances of success go way up if you're not doing it alone.

Chapter 13

MEDICATION

By now you might have concluded that you have ADHD, having recognized yourself in this book, and be wondering whether that means you're supposed to take medication. You may be cracking a smile because someone close to you has been encouraging you to try medication for years. Or you may be frowning because you don't like the idea of taking medication.

In this chapter, I'm going to shine a light on the facts about ADHD medication and answer some common questions so you can make the best decision for yourself.

What drugs are used to treat ADHD?

Medication is what I call "the most powerful tool everyone fears", and that's the truth.

Used properly, medication for ADHD can be a godsend, improving your mental focus, giving you greater control over your runaway brain, reducing your impulsivity thus helping you look before you leap, and helping you feel more in control and therefore less anxious.

The main class of medication used to treat ADHD is stimulant medication. The first stimulant used to treat what we now call ADHD was amphetamine. In 1937, psychiatrist Charles Bradley gave amphetamine to the hyperactive boys on his hospital ward. The boys were glad to take the medication, calling it their "arithmetic pill" because it enabled them to focus on learning their infernally boring maths facts.

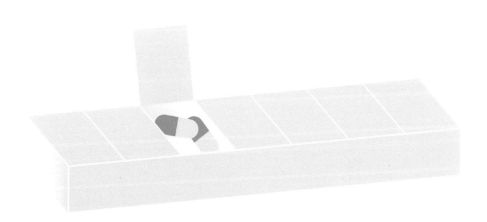

In the early 1950s, methylphenidate came on the scene. It's a different molecule than amphetamine, but it has the same therapeutic action, namely, to enhance focus and assist in controlling behaviour.

Amphetamine and methylphenidate form the two pillars of stimulant medication and have spawned numerous offspring stimulant medications. Some act over a long period of time (8–14 hours), others over a shorter period (3–5 hours). Some come in liquid form, some are tablets or capsules. Some need to be dissolved under the tongue. Some are used to saturate a patch that can be applied to the skin. There's even one that is taken at bedtime and only becomes active when you wake up in the morning, thus allowing you to avoid the hellish wait for the medication to kick in. The types of medicine licensed for the treatment of ADHD varies from country to country. Your doctor will advise you on the best available medications for you.

No form of medication continues to be prescribed over such a long period of time unless it is both safe and effective. Since 1937, a vast array of studies, articles, and books have made stimulants one of the most thoroughly investigated medications we use.

Keep in mind

Stimulant medication should only be taken under medical supervision.

Frequently asked questions

Below are a few of the most common questions I am asked about ADHD medication.

Is ADHD medication addictive?

One of the many myths about stimulant medication is that it is addictive. Research has shown that stimulant medication actually reduces the rate of addiction. By taking the right medication you become far less tempted to use the wrong medication.

The reason many people who fall into the trap commonly called addiction (see Chapter 8, pages 122–141) is because they are self-medicating untreated ADHD with their substance or behaviour of choice. By taking stimulant medication they stand a reasonable chance of ending their unhealthy addiction.

How does stimulant medication work?

How can a stimulant be good for an adult who has ADHD? Aren't people with ADHD already overstimulated? The resolution of this paradox lies in understanding what the stimulant medications stimulate. They stimulate the brain's inhibitory neurons. It's like putting on the brakes, stimulating the neurons that can slow down the runaway brain.

Stimulant medications work by increasing the level of certain chemicals, called neurotransmitters, in your brain. The most important ones these medications impact are dopamine, epinephrine (also known as adrenaline), and norepinephrine (noradrenaline). The neurotransmitters help sort out the many traffic jams that ADHD causes in the brain's circuitry.

What are the possible side effects of stimulants?

Medication is just one tool in the toolbox for helping adults with ADHD. It can be a godsend for some people (of all ages), ineffective for others, and fraught with unpleasant side effects for still others.

One side effect that usually occurs with the stimulant medications used to treat ADHD is the suppression of appetite. However, as long as you take care not to lose more weight than is good for you, that's an acceptable side effect.

All the other potential side effects are immediately reversible by lowering the dose or discontinuing the medication altogether. These potential side effects include elevated blood pressure, elevated heart rate, headaches, dry mouth, and, if you take the pill too close to bedtime, insomnia. In addition, some people simply do not like how the medication makes them feel, as if they'd lost their zest or spontaneity. If that happens, you simply stop the medication and you go back to your regular self.

Keep in mind

Do you remember how I compared the ADHD brain to a Ferrari with bicycle brakes (see page 24)? Well, ADHD medication can help strengthen your brakes, giving you greater control over your brain so you can win races instead of spinning out on curves.

Are there alternatives to stimulants?

If for any reason a person does not want to take a stimulant or they've tried the stimulants without success, then there are several categories of medication that can work just as well. As I said, it all comes down to trial and error.

Among the non-stimulants, SNRI (selective norepinephrine reuptake inhibitors) antidepressants, such as atomoxetine, are the most common. Guanfacine, an alpha-blocker, or alpha2A-adrenergic receptor agonist, is another non-stimulant medication prescribed for ADHD.

Keep in mind

The results of taking medication are reversible, not irreversible like surgery. Whatever the medication does is gone as soon as it washes out of your system, which is usually the same day you take it.

About 70% of the time, you can find a medication that works

Is ADHD medication the right choice for me?

No one has to take medication for ADHD. It is optional rather than a medical necessity.

The best way to find out which, if any, medication is best for you, and at what dose, is trial and error. We're not yet at the stage of having a test, genetic or otherwise, that will tell us which medication will work best for an individual. But since the most common medications we use to treat ADHD are fast-acting, in and out of your system the same day, it is possible to go through quite a few trials in a short period of time.

One of the most common reasons for medication failure is giving up too soon or not taking a high enough dose. As long as you don't see side effects, you can keep increasing the dose until you see the improvement you're hoping for.

With trial and error, you can find a medication that works about 70 per cent of the time. By "works" I mean you get target symptom improvement with no side effects (other than appetite suppression without unwanted weight loss).

Keep in mind

Living with untreated ADHD is like driving a car on square wheels. When you find the right medication for you, it rounds out the wheels, allowing you to go a lot further with a lot less effort.

Understanding your options

As you can see, there are many medications to choose from, which is great. However, that abundance of choice underlines just how important it is to work with an expert who knows the ins and outs of those medications. Find a prescriber who has a good knowledge of ADHD, someone who has treated lots of people with ADHD and who understands all the various treatments on offer, including medication.

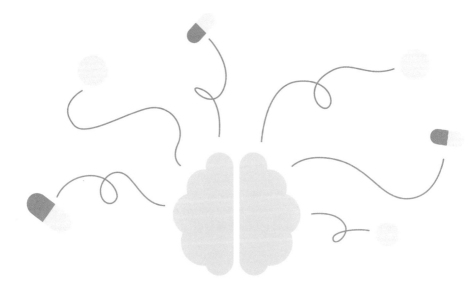

The bottom line

The entire matter of medication comes down to this: if you try a medication and it helps you without causing any side effects, be glad and continue to take it for as long as you like. If it does not help you, or it does cause side effects, then stop the medication and consult with your doctor to decide on next steps.

Or to put it even more succinctly: if you like it, take it; if you don't, don't.

But remember also, you should make these decisions and determinations in cooperation with a prescriber who's been around the block more than a few times.

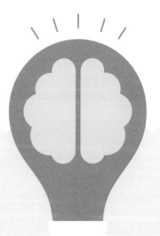

Keep in mind

Medication should never be the sole treatment. It should always be combined with learning about yourself, your version of ADHD and ADHD in the widest sense, and healthy living (see pages 184–203).

A final word

Here we are at the end of the book. Thank you for your participation. Without you, my work has no meaning, so my thanks couldn't be more sincere.

Although I don't know you personally, you've been on my mind every page of the way. I hope I've introduced you to the glories and the pitfalls in the world of ADHD. I hope I've taken you beyond the trivializing stereotypes and shown you the immense variety inherent in this fascinating condition so misleadingly called ADHD. I also hope I've shown you enough about the world of ADHD that you can feel proud if you have it.

And I hope I've armed you with all the information you need in order to avoid the traps you might otherwise fall into.

If you have learned anything of value in these pages, please tell others. Word of mouth is the best tool we have to combat stigma and spread the good news about this condition.

Thank you for taking this ride with me. Please do drop in and see me some time. You can find me at drhallowell.com/watch/ned-talks.

Resources

Organizations dedicated fully or partially to ADHD

Australia

ADHD Support Australia
(adhdsupportaustralia.com.au)

ADHD Foundation (adhdfoundation.org.au)

Canada

Centre for ADHD Awareness, Canada (caddac.ca)

Ireland

ADHD Ireland (adhdireland.ie)

New Zealand

ADHD New Zealand (adhd.org.nz)

UK

ADHD Foundation, The Neurodiversity Charity
(adhdfoundation.org.uk)

Attention Deficit Disorder Information and Support
Service (addiss.co.uk)

UK ADHD Partnership (ukadhd.com)

UK Adult ADHD Network (ukaan.org)

USA

American Academy of Child and Adolescent
Psychiatry (aacap.org)

American Psychiatric Association (psychiatry.org)

American Psychological Association (apa.org)

Attention Deficit Disorder Association (add.org)

Children and Adults with Attention-Deficit/
Hyperactivity Disorder (chadd.org)

Web resources

ADDConsults (addconsults.com)

ADDitude (additudemag.com)

Faster than Normal (fasterthannormal.com)

How to ADHD
(howtoadhd.com; youtube.com/howtoadhd)

Tracy Otsuka (Tracyotsuka.com)

Suggested reading

Barkley, Russell A., and Christine M. Benton PhD,
Taking Charge of Adult ADHD (Guildford Press,
2010).

Boissiere, Phil, MFT, *Thriving with Adult ADHD: Skills
to Strengthen Executive Functioning (Althea Press,
2018).*

Brown, Richard P., MD, and Patricia L. Gerbarg, MD
*Non-Drug Treatments for ADHD: New Options for
Kids, Adults, and Clinicians* (W.W. Norton &
Company, 2012).

Christakis, Nicholas A., MD, PhD, and James H.
Fowler, PhD, *Connected: The Surprising Power of
Our Social Networks and How They Shape Our
Lives* (New York: Little, Brown & Company, 2009).

Foote, Jeffrey, PhD, Carrie Wilkens, PhD, and Nicole
Kosanke, PhD *Beyond Addiction: How Science and
Kindness Help People Change* (New York: Scribner,
2014).

Frates, Beth, MD, Michelle Tollefson, MD, and Amy Comander, MD, *Paving the Path to Wellness Workbook* (Healthy Learning, 2021).

Hallowell, Edward M. MD, and John J. Ratey, MD, *ADHD 2.0: New Science and Essential Strategies for Thriving with Distraction from Childhood Through Adulthood* (Ballantine Books, 2021).

Matlen, Terry, MSW, *The Queen of Distraction: How Women with ADHD Can Conquer Chaos, Find Focus, and Get More Done* (New Harbinger Publications, 2014).

Ratey, John J., MD, and Eric Hagerman, *Spark! The Revolutionary New Science of Exercise and the Brain* (Quercus, 2009).

Shankman, Peter, *Faster than Normal: Turbocharge Your Focus, Productivity, and Success with the Secrets of the ADHD Brain* (TarcherPerigee, 2017).

Solden, Sari, MS, and Michelle Frank, PsyD, *A Radical Guide for Women with ADHD: Embrace Neurodiversity, Live Boldy, and Break Through* (New Harbinger Publications, 2019).

Walker, Matthew, PhD, *Why We Sleep: Unlocking the Power of Sleep and Dreams* (Scribner, 2017).

Data credits

Page 9: Barbaresi W.J., Katusic S.K., Colligan R.C., et al., "How common is attention-deficit/hyperactivity disorder? Incidence in a population-based birth cohort in Rochester, Minn.", *Arch Pediatr Adolesc Med.* 2002;156(3):217-224. doi:10.1001/archpedi.156.3.217.

Page 12: Rodden, Janice, "ADHD May Reduce Life Expectancy by As Much As 13 Years", *ADDitude* (20 November 2018), additudemag.com/adhd-life-expectancy-russell-barkley, accessed 27 February 2023.

Page 33: Zametkin A.J., Nordahl T.E., Gross M., et al., "Cerebral glucose metabolism in adults with hyperactivity of childhood onset", *N Engl J Med.* 1990;323(20):1361-1366. doi:10.1056/NEJM199011153232001. Copyright © 1990

Massachussetts Medical Society. Reprinted with permission from Massachussetts Medical Society.

Pages 35-37: Reprinted with permission from the *Diagnostic and Statistical Manual of Mental Disorders*, 5th edition, text revision, DSM-V-TR, pp. 68-70 (Copyright ©2022). American Psychiatric Association. All Rights Reserved.

Page 42: Smith M., "Hyperactive Around the World? The History of ADHD in Global Perspective", *Soc Hist Med.* 2017;30(4):767-787. doi:10.1093/shm/hkw127.

Page 42: Barbaresi W.J., Katusic S.K., Colligan R.C., et al., "How common is attention-deficit/hyperactivity disorder? Incidence in a population-based birth cohort in Rochester, Minn.", *Arch Pediatr Adolesc Med.* 2002;156(3):217-224. doi:10.1001/archpedi.156.3.217.

Page 46: Slobodin O., Davidovitch M., "Gender Differences in Objective and Subjective Measures of ADHD Among Clinic-Referred Children", *Front Hum Neurosci.* 2019;13:441. Published 2019 Dec 13. doi:10.3389/fnhum.2019.00441.

Page 46: American Psychiatric Association, *Diagnostic and Statistical Manual of Mental Disorders*, 5th edition, text revision, DSM-V-TR (American Psychiatric Association, 2022), p. 72.

Page 47: Stibbe T., Huang J., Paucke M., Ulke C., Strauss M., "Gender differences in adult ADHD: Cognitive function assessed by the test of attentional performance", *PLoS One.* 2020;15(10):e0240810. Published 2020 Oct 15. doi:10.1371/journal.pone.0240810.

Page 95: Beauchaine T.P., Ben-David I., Bos M., "ADHD, financial distress, and suicide in adulthood: A population study", *Sci Adv.* 2020;6(40):eaba1551. Published 2020 Sep 30. doi:10.1126/sciadv.aba1551.

Page 96: Pelham W.E. III, Page T.F., Altszuler A.R., Gnagy E.M., Molina B.S.G., Pelham W.E. Jr, "The long-term financial outcome of children diagnosed with ADHD", *J Consult Clin Psychol.* 2020;88(2):160-171. doi:10.1037/ccp0000461.

Page 96: Jones, Rupert, "Shopping is a nightmare: how ADHD affects people's spending habits", *The Guardian* (25 Jun 2022).

Page 109: John Gabrieli; McGovern Institute; Grover Hermann Professor, Health Sciences and Technology; Professor, Brain and Cognitive Sciences; Director, Athinoula A. Martinos Imaging Center, MIT.

Page 112: Csikszentmihalyi, Mihalyi, *Flow: The Psychology of Optimal Experience* (Harper 2008).

Page 126: Facher, Lev, "Rahul Gupta, first physician to serve as drug czar, says stigma among doctors is key culprit in addiction crisis", *Stat* (2 September 2022), statnews.com/2022/09/02/rahul-gupta-drug-czar-says-stigma-among-doctors-adds-to-addiction-crisis, accessed 27 February 2023.

Page 126: National Center for Drug Abuse Statistics (drugabusestatistics.org), accessed 27 February 2023.

Page 126: The UK Drug and Alcohol Survey of 2021, delamere.com/blog/the-uk-drug-and-alcohol-use-survey-2021, accessed 27 February 2023.

Page 128: Kelly, A.B., et al., "The Age of Onset of Substance Use Disorders", in de Girolamo, G., et al, (eds), *Age of Onset of Mental Disorders* (Springer, 2019).

Page 130: Waldinger, Robert, M.D., *The Good Life: Lessons from the World's Longest Scientific Study on Happiness* (Simon & Schuster, 2023).

Page 133: Blum, Kenneth, PhD, *Alcohol and the Addictive Brain* (Free Press, 1991).

Page 144: Waldinger, Robert, M.D., *The Good Life: Lessons from the World's Longest Scientific Study on Happiness* (Simon & Schuster, 2023).

Page 145: Vaillant, George, M.D., *Aging Well: Surprising Guideposts to a Happier Life, from the Landmark Harvard Study of Adult Development* (Little, Brown Spark, 2003).

Page 146: Murthy, Vivek, M.D., *Together: The Healing Power of Connection in a Sometimes Lonely World* (Harper Wave, 2020).

Page 146: Berkman, Lisa, "Social Networks, Support, and Health: Taking the Next Step Forward", *American Journal of Epidemiology*. 1986; 123(4):559–562. doi.org/10.1093/oxfordjournals.aje. a114276.

Page 146: Holt-Lunstad J., Smith T.B., Baker M., Harris T., Stephenson D., "Loneliness and social isolation as risk factors for mortality: a meta-analytic review", *Perspect Psychol Sci.* 2015;10(2):227-237. doi:10.1177/1745691614568352.

Page 177: Arthur C. Brooks, "The Secret to Happiness at Work", *The Atlantic* (2 September 2021), theatlantic.com/family/archive/2021/09/dream-job-values-happiness/619951, accessed 27 February 2023.

Page 177: Arvey, Richard D., et al., "Job Satisfaction: Environmental and Genetic Components", *Journal of Applied Psychology*, April 1989; 74(2):187-192. doi:10.1037/0021-9010.74.2.187.

Page 180: Arthur C. Brooks, "4 Rules for Identifying Your Life's Work", *The Atlantic* (21 May 2020), theatlantic.com/family/archive/2020/05/how-choose-fulfilling-career/611920, accessed 27 February 2023.

Page 186: Fatma Al-Maskeri, MBChB, PhD, LRCP&SI, FFPH, "Lifestyle Diseases: An Economic Burden on the Health Services", *U.N. Chronicle* (27 June 2013).

Page 199: Zylowska, Lidia, M.D., *The Mindfulness Prescription for ADHD* (Trumpeter, 2012).

Index

achievement drive 23
  see also underachievement
ADD see attention deficit
  disorder
addiction 12, 23, 47, 58, 122–41
  action plan for 136–40
  behavioural 129, 134–5
  and disconnection 74
  and dopamine 134–5
  and medication 208
  seduction of 124–6
  "trap model" 123, 124, 134–6,
    138, 165, 208
ADHD see attention deficit
  hyperactivity disorder
ADHD coaches 70, 102, 139,
  202–3
ADHD experts 68–9
ADHD people 11, 29, 40–51
ADHD plan 16, 66–79
  and ADHD coaches 70
  and ADHD experts 69
  and creative outlets 76
  and employment 75
  and learning about ADHD 68
  and lifestyle checklists 72
  and medication trials 77
  and romantic partners 75
  and social connection 74
  and structure 71
  and support 73
Adler, Len 46
adrenaline (epinephrine) 82, 194,
  208
alcohol consumption 58
  and addiction 23, 128

and moderation 197
and sleep 193
and "The Itch" 165
Alcoholics Anonymous 140
alienation 74, 119
alpha2A-adrenergic receptor
  agonists 210
alpha-blockers 210
amphetamines 45, 206–7
ancient Greeks 44, 116
antidepressants 10, 47, 210
anxiety 12, 47, 49–50, 58
  and complete diagnoses 136
  and creativity 109
  and disconnection 74
  and medication 206
  and money matters 96, 98–9
  and physical exercise 194
  and the Worry and Anxiety
    Equation 100–1
appetite suppression 209
appointments 90
arguments 158
Atlantic, The (magazine) 177,
  180
attention 19, 20
  and the default mode
    network 110, 114–17, 119
  "diseases of" 45
  redirecting 114–17, 119–20
  see also inattention
attention deficit disorder (ADD)
  20, 45, 46
attention deficit hyperactivity
  disorder (ADHD)
  ADHD, combined type 20, 37

ADHD, primarily hyperactive
  type 20, 37
ADHD, primarily inattentive
  type 20, 37
caricature 14
definition 18–39
diagnosis 9, 10, 17
explaining 18–39
as "fake" diagnosis 30, 33
history of 44
learning how to control 24–5,
  68, 166, 206, 208–9
misunderstandings about 14,
  58
negative attributes 12–14, 16,
  54–9, 64–5, 92–105, 106–21,
  178
positive attributes 14–16, 54–7,
  60–1, 64–5, 178
prevalence 42–3
stigma of 14
subtypes 20, 37
symptoms 19, 35–7
undiagnosed 9, 12–13, 17, 26–7,
  46–7, 58–9
untreated 32, 58–9, 68, 211
ways of being 22–3
attitude 188–9
autism spectrum disorder 109
automatic writing 171
avoidance behaviours 98–101,
  105, 129

Barkley, Russell 12
behavioural addictions 129,
  134–5

Berkman, Lisa 146
bipolar disorder 49, 109
blame, externalization 159
blood pressure 192, 209
Blum, Kenneth 133
body weight 187, 209
    see also obesity
borderline personality 109
boredom 23, 115
    and challenges 174
    and lack of structure 63
    and money matters 98, 100
    and self-care 185, 187
Bradley, Charles 45, 206
brain 21, 192
    and addiction 134
    and ADHD differences 33
    connectomes of 109, 110
    Ferrari metaphor 24–5
    and medication 208, 209
    and physical exercise 195
    reward system 134
    runaway 24–5, 166, 206,
        208–9
    and sleep 131
brain scans 109
Branson, Richard 11
breathwork 190–1, 198–200
brooding 107, 110
Brooks, Arthur C. 177, 180

cancer 186
careers 59, 75, 176–83
    and being true to yourself 183
    finding the right job 178–9
    four steps to 180
    and "hard work" 33
    and play 180, 181–3
    see also unemployment
cerebellum 195
challenges 174–5
child psychiatrists 69
children
    diagnosis 35–7
    "nervous" 45
chronic obstructive pulmonary
    disease (COPD) 186

coenzymes 194
cognitive impairment 20
composition 171
compulsions 23
concentration 194
connectomes 109, 110–12, 114–19
    see also default mode
        network; task positive
        network
conscious mind 167
contentment 115
control issues 100–1, 169
cooking 173
COPD see chronic obstructive
    pulmonary disease
coping mechanisms 98–101
cravings 135
creativity 23, 41, 55, 61, 162–75
    lack of 170–3
    and mental disorders 109
    outlets for 76, 130, 163, 171–2,
        174
    and play 181
    process of 168–9
    recognition of your 166–7
    "sing when you ping"
        approach to 132, 168
    and "The Itch" 76, 163–5, 168,
        174
Crichton, Alexander 45
crises 63
Csikszentmihalyi, Mihaly 112
cultural values 33
curiosity 55

dairy-free foods 197
danger-seeking 134
deadlines 72, 82
death, premature 12–13, 99, 146,
    186–7
default mode network (DMN)
    110–12, 198
    learning to control 114–21, 168,
        183
default rate 95
defensiveness 152
delegation 103

denial 98–9
depression 10, 12, 47, 49–50, 58
    and complete diagnoses 136
    and creativity 109, 130
    and disconnection 74
    and loneliness 146
    and money issues 96
    and physical exercise 194
    and sleep 192
determination 178
diabetes, adult-onset 186
diagnosis of ADHD 46–7, 90, 136
    and addiction 136
    and ADHD experts 69
    adult 27, 35–7, 69
    boundaries of 50–1
    differential 49
    entire/complete 47, 136
    "fake" diagnosis concept 30,
        33
    presentations with few
        symptoms 48–9
    reductionist nature 34, 50
Diagnostic and Statistical
    Manual of Mental Disorders
    (DSM) 21, 23, 34, 35, 46, 48, 50,
    166
diagnostic criteria 35, 42
disconnection 74, 139, 146
    see also social isolation
disease, lifestyle-related 186–7
dishonesty 159
distractibility 35, 55, 86
distraction tasks 117
DMN see default mode network
dogs 73, 131, 152
doom and gloom 106–21, 168
dopamine 134–5, 194, 208
dopamine D2 receptors 133
drawing 171
dream journals 172
drug abuse 23, 58, 123, 128, 165
DSM see Diagnostic and
    Statistical Manual of Mental
    Disorders
dyslexia 28, 47
dysthymia 49

earnings 96
Edison, Thomas 33
education 68, 128, 138, 213
emotions 95, 132–3, 192, 195
    see also doom and gloom;
        feelings; specific emotions
empathy 138
encouragement 70
engagement 112
Epictetus 116
epinephrine (adrenaline) 82, 194,
    208
executive functioning (EF) 70, 94,
    102, 139, 157

facts 101
famous ADHD people 11
fantasies 173
fatigue 61
fear 150
    see also terror
feelings 101
    see also doom and gloom;
        emotions
financial advisors 102
"flow" 112
flower arranging 172
fMRI see functional magnetic
    resonance imaging
focus 91, 95, 206–7
food addiction 23, 129, 134, 196
friends 73, 117, 202–3
frontal lobes 195
functional magnetic resonance
    imaging (fMRI) 109

Gabrieli, John 109
gambling addiction 23, 58, 129,
    134, 165
gender issues 19, 46, 58
general practitioners (GPs) 69
genes 124
genetics 19, 28, 133, 177
glucose uptake 33
gluten-free foods 197
Google 68
gratitude practice 132

guanfacine 210
guilt 185

happiness 116, 130, 132, 145
"hard work" 33
Harvard Study of Adult
    Development 144–5
health 184–203
    and attitude 188–9
    importance of 186–7
    and lifestyle factors 190–200
    and mental health 191
    motivation for 202–3
    neglect of 99
    personalized 201
    plans for 201, 202
heart disease 186
help-seeking 85, 89, 101, 103, 105,
    126
high blood pressure 192
Hilton, Paris 11
Hippocrates 44
honesty, culture of 128
HOPE method 70
hormones 194
hydration 197
hyperactivity 19, 20, 35
    and medication 206
    symptoms of 36, 37, 46, 48
hyperexcitability 45
hyperfocus 91
hyperkinetic reaction of
    childhood 45
hypermetamorphosis 45
hypocrisy 23

ideas 183
imagination 61
    and creativity 76, 168–9, 174
    and the default mode
        network 111, 121, 183
    and flow 112
    lack of 183
    and love 149
    and play 181–3
    and the task positive network
        111, 112

immune function 192
impatience 23
impulsivity 19, 35, 55
    and creativity 166
    and flow 112
    and medication 206
    symptoms of 36, 46, 48
inattention 19, 35, 37, 46, 48
injury 12
insomnia 209
inspiration 164
intention, communicating your
    158
"Itch, The" (creative impulse) 76,
    163–5, 168, 174

job satisfaction 177

lateness 83–91
law-breaking 74
laziness 30, 33
letting go 169
lifestyle
    checklist 72
    and health 190–200
    -related disease 186–7
listening skills 160
loans 95
Locke, John 44
loneliness 146
    see also disconnection; social
        isolation
love 130, 143, 144–5, 148–9
    and happiness 145
    and health 191
    informed 141
    obstacles to 150
    opening yourself up to 152
    taking a risk on 152, 161
    see also self-love
lying 159

managing ADHD 25, 58, 78
    see also medication
Martian test 38
MAT see medication-assisted
    treatment

Mayo Clinic 42
meal-skipping 197
medication 16, 204–13
    and addiction 208
    and doom and gloom 119
    failure 211
    frequently asked questions
        regarding 208–11
    mode of action 208
    non-stimulant 210
    and punctuality 90
    reversible nature 210
    side effects 209, 211, 213
    stimulant 10, 77, 95, 140,
        206–10
    trialling 77, 211
medication-assisted treatment
    (MAT) 140
meditation 136, 190–1, 198–9
memory 194
mental health, and physical
    health 191
mental wellbeing 72, 184–203
metabolic syndrome 186
methylphenidate 207
micronutrients 133
mind
    conscious 167
    racing 23, 100–1
    unconscious 167–9, 171
mindfulness 190–1, 198–9
missions, personal 61
mistakes made by ADHD
    people, learning not to take
    personally 157
misunderstandings 158
misunderstood feelings 157
mobile phones 193
moderation
    and alcohol 197
    modelling 128
money management issues 12,
    92–105
mood, low 132–3
mood-boosters 130–1
moral control, abnormal defects
    of 45

"muse" 164
music 117, 171

narcissism 109
Narcotics Anonymous 140
"nature vs nurture" 177
Neeleman, David 11
"nervous children" 45
neurologists 69
neurons 109–10, 131, 194
    inhibitory 208
neuroscience 109
neurotransmitters 134–5, 208
    see also specific
        neurotransmitters
New England Journal of
    Medicine 33
nicotine 23
norepinephrine (noradrenaline)
    194, 208
nutrition 72, 133, 136, 187, 190–1,
    196–7

obesity 186
optimism 138
organizational difficulties 93, 195
originality 23, 61, 169

pain, preference for 115, 116
pain relief
    and addiction 123–4, 127–9,
        138, 140
    healthy routes to 127, 129–31,
        136
Palmer, Christopher 191
PAM see precision addiction
    management
paranoia 109
partners 75, 154–5
passions 148–9, 180
passive-aggression 87
peptides 194
pets 73, 131, 152
photography 172
physical exercise 72, 187, 190–1,
    194–5
    addiction 117, 129, 134

as healthy coping mechanism
    130, 136
    personalized plans for 201
piano playing 171
planning 195
    and addiction 136–40
    difficulties with 93
    and health 201, 202
    and money issues 101
play 180, 181–3
pleasure-seeking
    and addiction 123–4, 127–9,
        140
    and dopamine 134–5
    healthy routes 127, 130–1, 136,
        138
    and reward deficiency
        syndrome 132–3
positive focus 115, 116
post-traumatic stress disorder
    (PTSD) 49, 136
precision addiction
    management (PAM) 133
priorities 71
problem-solving 88
procrastination 86, 186
psychoanalysis 119
psychologists 69
psychosis 37
punctuality 83–91
punishment 128
puzzles 117

record-keeping 104
reframing 85
rejection sensitive dysphoria 136
relationships 75, 130, 142–61
    difficulties 12, 58, 74
    see also love; social
        connection
religion 119
repellent personalities 129
"rescuers" 61, 155
review writing 173
reward deficiency syndrome
    132–3
reward system 134

right, being 159
"right difficult" 76, 174, 175, 180
risk-taking 128
role playing 128
routines 193
rules, not playing by the 23

schizophrenia 37
school 11, 58
science 33
screaming 117
screen addiction 129, 134
scripts, "can-do" 189
selective norepinephrine
    reuptake inhibitors (SNRIs) 210
self, being true to your 183
self-care 71
    neglect 12, 185
    see also health; wellbeing
self-esteem 58, 107, 178
self-harm 23
self-love 138
self-medication 58, 82, 196, 208
self-talk see voices, inner
sex
    addiction 23, 58, 129, 134
    casual 165
    scheduling time for 71
shame 104–5, 124, 126, 138
shopping addiction 23, 58, 129,
    134
sleep 71–2, 131, 136, 190–3
Smalley, Susan 199
smoking 186, 187
SNRIs see selective
    norepinephrine reuptake
    inhibitors
social connection 74, 142–61
    and addiction 130, 136, 139,
        141
    and finding the right partner
        154–5
    obstacles to 150, 156–60
    and opening yourself up to
        love 152
    power of 144–5
    through food 197

through work 177
    see also disconnection;
        friends; love; relationships
social isolation 74, 118, 129, 146
    see also disconnection
spending addiction 23, 58, 129,
    134
spontaneity 25
stigma 14, 126, 138
Still, George 45
stimulant medication 10, 77, 95,
    140, 206–10
stimulation seeking 20, 23, 61–3,
    128
    and the default mode
        network 115–17
    and employment 180
    and money issues 98
    and partner choice 155
    and punctuality 89
    and sleep 131
Stoics 116
stress relief 127
stroke 186
structure 61–3, 71, 86
stubbornness 23, 61
"stuck" people 41
substance abuse 165
    see also alcohol
        consumption; drug abuse
substance use disorder (SUD) 47,
    49, 109, 126, 128, 134
successful ADHD people 11, 29
sugar addiction 23, 196
suicide 74, 96, 118
support 202–3
    see also friends; social
        connection
survival instinct 78
synapses 134, 194

talking things through 73
task positive network (TPN)
    110–12, 120
teamwork 202–3
teenagers 128
terror 98, 100

see also fear
therapists 139
"thrival instinct" 78
time, distorted sense of 23,
    80–91
TPN see task positive network
traits 20–1
trauma 136
twin studies 177

unconscious mind 167–9, 171
underachievement 10–12, 17, 23,
    26–8, 41, 58
underperformance 59
unemployment 12, 74

Vaillant, George 145
values, cultural 33
variability 20
variable attention stimulation
    trait (VAST) 20
viral infections 192
Vitamin Connect 197, 201
voice, inner
    negative 108–9, 188–9
    positive 189
vulnerability 100–1, 152, 161

water intake 197
weight loss 209
wellbeing 72, 184–203
wholefoods 197
will.i.am 11
willpower 124
withdrawal 135
women, with ADHD 46–7, 58
World Health Organization
    (WHO) 186
worriers 170
Worry and Anxiety Equation
    100–1
writing 90, 171, 173

Zylowska, Lidia 199

Acknowledgements

Like almost every author, I have more people to thank than space to thank them. Nonetheless, here goes anyway, starting with you, the reader: thank you.

Thank you to the brilliant Zara Anvari, who conceived this book and then asked me to write it. And thanks to her entire team at DK, including Clare Churly, who kept me writing more briskly than I've ever written before, Izzy Holton, Becky Alexander, Tania Da Silva Gomes, Michelle Noel, and Katie Edmundson. I hope I've done you all justice.

Thank you to Jim Levine, my wonderful agent, and his team. What a luxury it is for me to have not just an agent, but a whole team of them. They are real pros who never quit; pulling me along like a team of huskies at the Iditarod Trail Sled Dog Race. They're always there when I need them, and when my spirits sag, they pick them up.

Finally, I would like to thank my sun, my moon, and my stars: my wife of 34 years, Sue, and our three children, Lucy, Jack, and Tucker. It seems like only yesterday that I was writing the acknowledgements for my first book, when my children were aged just six, three, and six months, but the calendar tells me that was 27 years ago. Although we've all grown a few years older since then, you guys will be my whole enchilada forever.

About the author

Dr Edward M. Hallowell is a board-certified child and adult psychiatrist, a world-renowned keynote speaker, and the *New York Times* bestselling author or co-author of more than 20 books including *Driven to Distraction* (co-authored with John J. Ratey), which sparked a revolution in our understanding of ADHD, and more recently *ADHD 2.0*. A regular columnist for *ADDitude* magazine, he also chronicles advice and personal experiences of ADHD as viral "Ned Talks" on TikTok. The founder of The Hallowell Centers in Boston, New York City, San Francisco, and Seattle, he still sees his private patients, the main source of all he knows, every day. He lives with his wife, a social worker, in the Boston area where, having launched their three grown children, they plan their next adventures.

Disclaimer

The information in this book has been compiled by way of general guidance in relation to the specific subjects addressed. It is not a substitute and not to be relied on for medical, healthcare, pharmaceutical, or other professional advice on specific circumstances and in specific locations. Please consult your GP before starting, changing, or stopping any medical treatment. So far as the author is aware, the information given is correct and up to date as of March 2023. Practice, laws, and regulations all change, and the reader should obtain up-to-date professional advice on any such issues. The naming of any product, treatment, or organization in this book does not imply endorsement by the author or publisher, nor does the omission of any such names indicate disapproval. The author and publisher disclaim, as far as the law allows, any liability arising directly or indirectly from the use, or misuse, of the information contained in this book.

Penguin Random House

DK LONDON
Senior Acquisitions Editor Zara Anvari, Becky Alexander
Project Editor Izzy Holton
Senior Designer Tania Gomes
Jacket Coordinator Jasmin Lennie
Production Editor David Almond
Senior Production Controller Stephanie McConnell
Art Director Maxine Pedliham
Publishing Director Katie Cowan

Editor Clare Churly
Design and Illustrations Studio Noel

First published in Great Britain in 2023 by
Dorling Kindersley Limited
DK, One Embassy Gardens, 8 Viaduct Gardens,
London, SW11 7BW

The authorised representative in the EEA is
Dorling Kindersley Verlag GmbH. Arnulfstr. 124, 80636
Munich, Germany

A CIP catalogue record for this book
is available from the British Library.
ISBN: 978-0-2416-3165-2

Printed and bound in Slovakia

For the curious
www.dk.com

MIX
Paper | Supporting
responsible forestry
FSC www.fsc.org
FSC™ C018179

This book was made with Forest Stewardship Council™ certified paper - one small step in DK's commitment to a sustainable future. **For more information go to www.dk.com/our-green-pledge**